From Acorı  Santry's ____

Published by: History Group, Santry Guild Irish Countrywomen's Association

ISBN: 978-0-9556008-0-7

AN CHOMHAIRLE OIDHREACHTA

THE HERITAGE COUNCIL

This publication has received support from the Heritage Council under the 2007 Publications Grant Scheme

TM Printing Ltd., Ennis, Co. Clare
November 2007

Foreword

The forerunner of this book was a combined effort by members of the Santry Guild of the Irish Countrywomen's Association (Bantracht na Tuaithe) to produce a body of work for submission to the ICA for an Arts Award. The format for the Local History Arts Award was stringent: maximum 12,000 words, outlined historical walk, famous people, family and place names defined. These lists are retained and may be found in this publication. Happily the Guild was rewarded with an Arts Award, scoring an excellent mark.

We were advised to publish the work, *"From Acorns to Oaks, Santry's Story"* and the many tasks necessary for printing were undertaken. Now that our efforts have borne fruit and our book is published we hope our task will be thought worthwhile.

The rich history of Santry, from the time of the Almanii tribe (the Sean Trabh) to the year 2002, has proved fascinating to those who worked so diligently on this book. We hope to promote an appreciation of the past and awaken an interest in our colourful heritage in future generations.

Má fhaigheann tú leathchuid den taitneamh as bheith ag léamh na staire seo agus a fuaireamar as í a scríobh, ansin ní bheidh ár gcuid oibre tar éis bheith in aisce.

Content

Section V

Personalities - past and present

Lord Mayors of Dublin

Section VI

Historic Walk

"To get to know even a small field is a lifetime's exploration"

Patrick Kavanagh ("My Three Books")
Kavanagh's Weekly, June 28, 1952
P.1.

Introduction

"**S**eantrabh"[1] (Santry) meaning "Old Tribe" lies 6 kms. north of Dublin city. The Swords Road, originally the "Royal Way"[2], dates from 1450 and runs through the heart of the Santry area. The M1 lies to the east and Ballymun Road to the west. The area of our study lies between these roads. It is bound by the Wad Stream, Shanowen Road to the south and the Cuckoo Stream, Toberbunny to the north. Our story begins in earliest times and ends at the beginning of the third millennium.

Earliest Times

Stone and Bronze Ages

Artefacts stored in the National Museum suggest that Stone and Bronze Age man lived in Santry. These include a polished stone axe-head[3] found in Santry demesne in 1947 and fragments of flint brass and bronze[4] unearthed in Santry during house building in 1969.

Bronze Tools

1

The Celts

Archaeologists believe that the Celts came to Ireland about 500 BC. The first Celtic settlement here dates from the early third century AD. Santry was then part of Magh Breagh, the plain of Bregia, a wide stretch of land extending from the river Liffey to Drumiskin, Co. Louth.

The first Celtic tribe in this area was called "Ciannachta"[5]. They were named after their chieftain Cian and were of Munster origin. Cormac MacAirt, High King of Ireland, granted the territory of Magh Breagh to Tadhg, son of Cian, as a reward for victory over the King of Ulster at the battle of Crinna, 226 AD.

The southern part of Magh Breagh, from the river Liffey to the river Delvin became known as Ard Ciannachta.

The Naniken river (Abha Chian), rises on the south side of Santry Avenue and flows under Santry village, past Magenta Hall on its way to Dublin Bay. This area kept the name Ard Ciannachta until Viking times when it became known as Fingal (the fair-haired Norsemen).

Earliest form of writing in Ireland was known as Ogham.
Consisted of lines carved at different angles on to large stones, as shown here.

2

The course of the Santry & Naniken rivers[6]

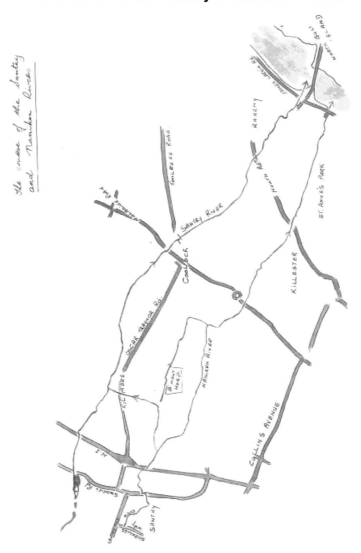

Courtesy of Dublin City Council
*Reproduced from the **"Rivers of Dublin"** by Clair L. Sweeney*

3

Christianity

After the arrival of St. Patrick in 432, Ireland converted to Christianity. In the sixth century a Christian settlement was established at Santry, on the Church of Ireland site. The 1936 Ordnance Survey map shows a curving enclosure around the church, indicating the existence of an early ecclesiastical settlement.

The monks in Santry lived in huts of clay and wattle and preached the gospel locally. They were cared for by the mother church in Swords. Their leader was Pappan who became patron of the area.

St. Pappan

St. Pappan was either son or grandson of Aengus MacNathfriach, King of Munster. He was educated at Glasnevin by St. Mobhi. His feast is celebrated on July 31st. According to tradition a patron in his honour was held annually, under an ancient tree in Poppintree. This ended in 1844.

Another Pappan?

St. Pappan is sometimes confused with another 'Pappan' [7], thought to have been born here, in the tenth century. He was believed to have emigrated to France where he built many churches. Rev. John Canon O'Hanlon in *'Lives of the Irish Saints'* [8] says that the second Pappan was born in Flanders in 978 and died at Stavelot, Belgium in 1048.

Santry Recorded

In the *'Annals of the Four Masters'* [9] 827 AD, the death of Cormac, son of Muirgheas, Abbot of Seantrabh is recorded. Soon afterwards the settlement was destroyed by the Vikings.

The Viking Era

While few traces of Viking occupation of Santry remain and no battles of note are recorded, Santry was clearly affected by the invasion of Fingal. It began in 795 with raids on coastal settlements at Lambay and Inishpatrick. St. Pappan's settlement was destroyed in 836 and not heard of again until 1038.

Viking Tools
*From **"Irish Lives"**, Allen Figgis & Co Ltd 1971*

Arrival of the Danes

The Danes reached Dublin in 847. According to *'Annals of the Four Masters'*, *"a great slaughter of the *Fingaill followed"*[10]. By 919 Danes and Vikings had made peace and were masters of Dublin City and Fingal. Danish occupation continued after the battle of Clontarf (1014).

Fingal was constantly attacked by neighbouring Celts. The death of Hamund MacTurkil, last Norse King of Dublin 1171, ended Viking power in Fingal. By then the Anglo-Normans had arrived.

*Fingaill=Vikings

Santry in Anglo-Norman Times
1169 – 1535

Henry I, Norman King of England, had his eyes on the rich lands of Ireland for some time. His opportunity to invade came in 1169 when Dermot McMurrough, King of Leinster, asked for help in his dispute with Tiernán O'Rourke, King of Breffni. By 1171, the Anglo-Normans were in possession of Fingal and in that year, the lands of Santry were granted to the Anglo-Norman, Adam de Phoepe.

Celtic Tuaths

Under the Anglo Normans, Celtic Tuaths became baronies. Baronies were sub-divided into parishes and parishes were further sub-divided into townlands. Santry, part of the Barony of Coolock, was declared a manor in 1376[11]. In that year, the manor was passed by Johanna, daughter of Francis de Phoepe, to Thomas Marewood later Baron of Skryne. Through marriage, the manor passed from the Marewood to the Nugent family of Rosse Castle, Co. Meath. William Nugent owned the lands at the time of the Reformation in 1535.

The Royal Way

The village dates from 1376 when it consisted of a number of thatched, whitewashed, mud-walled cabins[12]. The road through the village dates from 1450 when, according to a *'Chancery Note Roll'* of that date, it was known as *"The Royal Way"*, the route of the mail coach from Dublin to Derry and Belfast.

Mail Coach
From ***"Roads and Vehicles"*** by Anthony Bird 1900

The Church under the Anglo-Normans

At the time of the Anglo-Norman invasion, the Irish church was monastic and largely independent of Rome. Soon afterwards it changed to a parochial system with tithes payable to the Pope. In 1179, Pope Alexander III established forty parishes in Fingal. In the official church record of 1275, *'The Crede Mihi'*[13], Santry church is recorded as part of the Deanery of Swords with two dependant chapels: *"Ecclesia de Balgriffin* and *Ecclesia de Baldungan"*[14].

St. Pappan's - thirteenth century

Early in the thirteenth century, Adam de Phoepe built a church here dedicated to St. Pappan, described by Rev. John Canon O'Hanlon: as *"consisting of a chancel and nave separated or connected by a choir-arch"*[15]. Historians speculate as to whether the 'Pappan' de Phoepe had in mind was the eleventh century Abbot of Stavelot or the sixth century monk who established the original settlement.

This church was given to St. Mary's Abbey, Dublin. The monks of St. Mary's looked after the parishioners up to the time of the Reformation.

16th Century Font in St Pappan's church

Farming

The land acquired by the colonist was leased to the native Irish and rents collected. As the native population increased, demand for land grew and further leases were given by sub-dividing existing holdings. The land was farmed by colonist and native alike. Cereals were grown and cattle rearing practised. As early as 1285[16], corn from Santry was exported to Wales. Farming continued to be the main occupation up to the mid-twentieth century.

From the Reformation to the Barry Era
1535-1660

The Reformation

The Reformation in England began when Pope Clement VII refused to grant a divorce to Henry VIII. In 1534 the English Parliament declared Henry VIII supreme head of the church there and a similar Act was passed by the Irish Parliament in 1537. Two years later, William Landley, Abbot of St. Mary's Dublin, surrendered Santry Church to the Crown. Early in Elizabeth I's reign (1558 – 1603) St. Pappan's became a Protestant church[17].

Effects of the Reformation

Catholics refused to accept the authority of the crown or to attend church services run by ministers of the new religion. Santry church fell into disrepair. A report by the Protestant Archbishop of Dublin, Bulkeley, in 1630 said that: *"the church and chancel are uncovered_ _ _ and all parishioners save very few are recusants"* [18]. It suggested that Catholics from Santry attended Mass at Hollywood's Castle, Artane, where James Drake,

Roman Catholic Parish Priest of Artane, lived. According to Dr Joseph Donnelly in *'Short Histories of Dublin Parishes'* [19] nothing more is heard of religious practice in Santry until the end of the seventeenth century.

The Manor of Santry

William Nugent, whose family had owned the manor from 1535 onwards, lost his lands in 1575 for supporting the Irish side against Elizabeth I. According to B.W. Adams in *'History and description of Santry and Cloghran Parishes'* Elizabeth I leased *"The village of Santrieffe and the tythes of Dubber to Thomas 10th Earl of Ormond in 1575 for 60 years"* [20]. When Elizabeth I died in 1603, Ormond's lease was forfeited for non-payment of rents. James I restored Nugent's lands in 1608 and they remained with the Nugents until 1641 when they were lost for their part in the 1641 rebellion.

The Surveys of 1654 – 1656

Two surveys were taken about this time, The Down Survey and The Civil Survey. The Civil Survey details the lands of Santry held from 1641. The chief landowner was Sir James Barry, Protestant. His estate extended over: *"Santry, Ballystrowan, Silloge and Sterminstowne"* [21]

Other landowners were:

"Patricke Brymigan, Irish Papist, Dardistowne",

"Nick Hollywood of Artaine, Irish Papist, Hollywood's lands in Santrye",

"William Barry, Protestant, the forty acres – formerly Gouldings holding, Santry Village",

"James Barnwell of Dunbro, Protestant, Ballymon",

"The Minister of Santry – in Santyre – Gleabland" and

"Edward Barry, Protestant, Tobberbunny" [22].

Total acreage for the area of our study was 782 of which 685 were arable, 42 meadow, 39 pasture, 10 shrubwood and 6 ashgrove, showing that farming was fairly extensive.

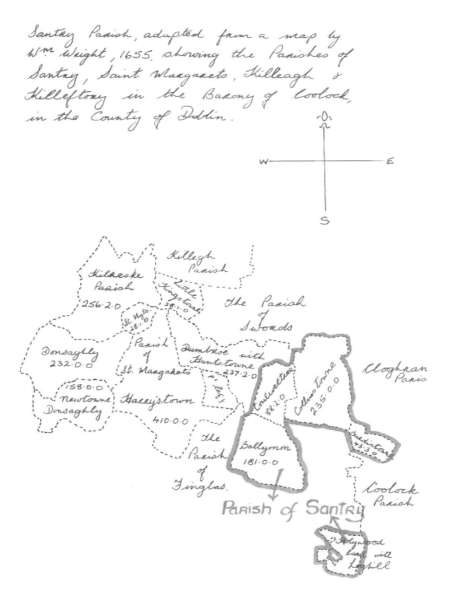

Santry Parish, adapted from a map by
W.m Wright, 1655, showing the Parishes of
Santry, Saint Margarets, Killeagh &
Killeftory in the Barony of Coolock,
in the County of Dublin.

Courtesy of National Library of Ireland

11

Battle of Santry 1641

Santry had its own little footnote in national history at this time. On the night of December 9th 1641 local men, both Catholics and Protestants were gathered in the village inn. The 1641 Rebellion against England had begun and Sir Charles Coote, leader of a group of English soldiers was on his way from Clontarf to Swords to disperse a group of Irish Rebels, led by Luke Netherville, who were assembled there.

En route to Swords he attacked the men gathered in Santry Inn on suspicion that they were rebels. The village was burnt and the heads of the murdered men were triumphantly carried on spikes into Dublin. This atrocity became known as the *'Battle of Santry'* [23].

The Barry Era
1660 – 1751

Who were the Barrys?

The Barrys came to Ireland at the time of the Anglo-Norman invasion from a place in Wales called 'Barri'. Philip de Barri got extensive grants of land in Co. Cork in 1179. Philip's family prospered and multiplied and several branches of the family formed septs in the Irish fashion. Sir James Barry, listed in the Civil Survey of 1654, was a descendant of this family. As well as their Santry estate, the Barrys were merchants and carried on their business at High Street, Dublin, where James Barry was born in 1603[24].

Santry Demesne
Picture courtesy of the National Library of Ireland

A Reward for Services Rendered

Sir James Barry advocated the restoration of the monarchy in Britain. In 1659, he became chairman of the Royalist Convention in Dublin, in defiance of the Government. When Charles II was restored to the throne in 1660, he appointed Sir James as Chief Justice of the King's Bench and Baron Barry of Santry. He took his seat as first Lord Santry in May 1661.

James Barry may have lived in the *"dwelling house of stone"* [25] in Santry, listed in the Civil Survey of 1654. He married Catherine, daughter of Lord Deputy Sir William Parsons. James died in February 1672 and was buried at Christchurch. He was succeeded by his eldest son, Richard, 2nd Lord Santry.

Richard Barry - 2nd Lord Santry

Richard married Elizabeth, daughter of Henry Jenery, of the Court of the King's Bench. He was a Protestant and did not sit in the parliament of the Roman Catholic King, James II, between 1685 –1688 [26]. During this time he lost his lands and title and lived in England. When James II's Protestant daughter, Mary, and her Dutch husband, William of Orange, took the throne of Britain in 1688, Richard had both his lands and title restored.

Richard's wife, Elizabeth, died in 1682 and he died in 1694. They were buried at Santry. The Barry tomb, erected in 1683, was situated near the entrance gate to St. Pappan's church. Richard was succeeded by his fourth eldest son, Henry.

Plaques in St Pappan's Church

Henry Barry - 3rd Lord Santry

Henry married Bridget, daughter of Thomas Domville, Templeogue. In 1702, he built Santry Court, a Queen Anne style four storey brick mansion, surrounded by 140 acres of parkland. The mansion, according to Samuel Lewis in *'A History and Topography of Dublin City and County'*, commanded *"some beautiful scenery and extensive mountain and sea views"*[27]. From this time onwards Santry Court became the focal point of the area.

New Church of St. Pappan

Under the direction of Henry, a new church was built on the old Celtic site in 1709. It was described by Rev. Robert Walsh in *'Fingal and its Churches'* as: *"a plain oblong quadrangular edifice, dedicated to St. Pappan. The western gable is surmounted by a double-arched bell turret"*[28]. The baptismal font from the thirteenth century church survived. This church is still in use today.

Registration of Catholic Priests

The Barrys were obviously closely involved in matters of Church and State. An Act of Parliament was passed in 1704, stating that only registered Catholic priests could practice. According to the *'Complete Peerage'*, the 3rd Lord Santry's signature, together with that of other notables, appeared on a document, dated August 17th 1719: *"seriously recommending the castration of all unregistered priests and friars, with a view to making the common Irish Protestants"*[29].

Henry died in 1734 and his wife, Bridget, died in 1750. They were buried at Santry. He was succeeded by his only son Henry.

A typical 16th century church
Picture courtesy of Irish Architectural Archives

Henry Barry - 4th: Lord Santry

Henry, 4th and last Lord Santry, born in 1710, died in exile in Nottingham in 1751[30]. With his death the peerage ended. Henry was such a colourful character that we have described his life in detail, among the personalities of the area. His will granted the lands of Santry to his uncle, Sir Compton Domville of Templeogue.

The Hell Fire Club Dublin (James Worsdale Artist) - Henry Barry First on Left
Courtesy of National Gallery of Ireland

Early Domvile Period
1751 – 1810

Who Were the Domviles?

The Domviles were descendants of William the Conqueror, first Norman King of England, who died in 1087. Gilbert Domvile came to Ireland from Lyme in Cheshire early in the seventeenth century. He settled at Loughlinstown in south County Dublin. His descendants acquired estates in north and south County Dublin and Queen's County as well as extensive properties in Dublin City.

(Note: The Domville family name has two spellings - "Domville" and "Domvile". Within this book we have used both versions)

Picture courtesy of Edward Alan Domville

Sir Compton Domvile

Sir Compton Domville, Templeogue, Privy Councillor and M.P. for County Dublin, succeeded to the Manor of Santry in 1751. He found that the Manor had been mortgaged by Henry Barry to Sir William Cooper for £1,640[31]. The lands were legally vested in the heiress of Sir William Cooper, Catherine Roth. As Catherine Roth was a minor, a Court Order was made empowering her to convey her legal interest in the estate to Sir Compton.

Sir Compton died, without heir, in 1768. He left his estate to his nephew, Charles Pocklington, M.P. of Scotland, on condition that he change his name to Domville.

Sir Compton Domvile, Bart
From a portrait in the procession of
Major H. W. Domvile

Taken from "History of Co. Dublin", *Part I by Francis Erlington Ball,
Published Dublin 1902*

Sir Charles Pocklington Domville

Charles was son of Christopher Pocklington and his wife Elizabeth Domville, second daughter of Thomas Domville of Templeogue. He showed little interest in his Santry estate and only moved there in 1780 when Templeogue House was falling into ruins. Charles married Margaret, daughter of Thomas Sheppard. Their son, Sir Compton Domville, inherited the estate in 1810.

Plaque in St Pappan's church dedicated to
Sir Charles Pocklington Domville
Margaret Sheppard -
Elizabeth Lindsay 1st wife of Sir Compton Domville
and the son of Sir Compton Domville and Lady Helena.

Beyond the Demesne Walls in the 18th / 19th Centuries

Poverty, vandalism and highway robbery were widespread in eighteenth and early nineteenth century Santry. Weston St. John Joyce in *'Neighbourhood of Dublin'*, tells us that the road between Drumcondra and Swords – The Great Northern Road: *"was one of the most dangerous in the metropolis"*[32]. Mail coaches, resting at the Royal Oak Inn, opposite Santry Demesne, were an easy target for robbers. The demesne, surrounded by a high wall, gave them an ideal hiding place.

'NINETY-EIGHT.—SIGNAL FOR THE OUTBREAK.
Attack on the Northern Mail Van at Santry, near Dublin, 23rd. May, 1798.

Picture courtesy of the National Library of Ireland

Highway Robbery

Between 1768 – 1777, five accounts of highway robbery were recorded. The appointment of a Parish Constable in 1785, made little difference. Political unrest made 1798 a particularly bad year. In March 1798, the North Mail, *en route* from Dublin, was attacked at Santry by a party of insurgents. Passengers' property and firearms valued at £400 were stolen. Two months later, the Belfast Mail was stopped in the village by armed men. Passengers were forced to alight and the coach was set on fire[33]. The flames, from the burning coach, were a pre-arranged signal for the 1798 rebellion in Fingal.

Yeomen

Next morning, Sir Henry Wilkinson, J.P. of Corballis, arrived in the village, with a party of yeomanry. They burnt a house in Chapel Lane. James Coughlan, landlord of the local public house and Laurence Mooney, a local man, were whipped for taking part in the previous day's incident, but the ringleaders escaped[34].

Royal Oak Inn

By this time, the Royal Oak Inn had closed. When Charles Kavanagh died in 1778, the licence was moved to a house in the village[35]. The Inn gave its name to Royal Oak farm, where farming continued for almost 200 years. Clay pipes, from the mail coach days were unearthed on the site during early 1980s.

Hard Times

A scarcity of fuel for fires caused a major problem for the poor. Fingal was without bogs and English coal was too expensive. People used whatever firewood came their way. Stealing timber became such a problem that a fund was set up in the Church in 1784. This fund, according to B. W. Adams: *"was for the prosecution of robbers and thieves, all cutters of timber and fences, robbers of gardens and stealers of gates and gateposts in the Parish of Santry and to award all those who shall be instrumental in bringing the offenders to punishment"* [36]. One church bell was stolen and bars were put on the belfry to protect the second one.

Sermons on behalf of the poor were preached in the church between 1778 and 1797, and money collected. Mrs. Wilmot of Dublin, left £10 in her will *"for the poor children of Santry"* [37]. This money was spent on clothes.

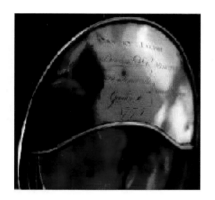

Alms Plate from St Pappan's Church[38]
(Purchased in 1776 for 13 Shillings)

The Manor Mill

During all this period of unrest, farming continued. The Manor Mill stood in the village near today's Allied Irish Bank. It stood there throughout the eighteenth century and was still in use when Colonel Joseph Archer surveyed the area in 1801[39]. Adams tells us that *"all tenants of the manor were bound by their leases to have their corn ground, paying toll to the lord of the manor for the mill part of his demesne"* [40].

Early 19th Century

In the early 19th century two highwaymen, Larry Clinch and Michael Collier operated in the area. Part of a ditch along the road, north of the entrance to Santry demesne, became known as Robbers' Bank.

Church at Santry, County of Dublin.

William Fredrick Wakeman – Artist (1822-1900)
Taken from "Lives of the Irish Saints" by Rev. John Canon O'Hanlon (C 1900)

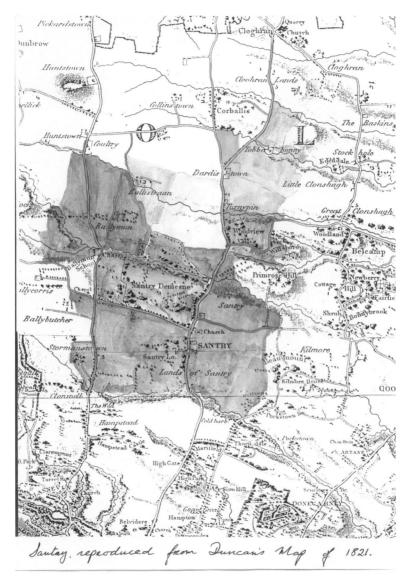

Santry, reproduced from Duncan's Map of 1821.

Another Ned Kelly?

Here Collier set up dummy figures, each held a *'gun'* to await the mail coach. Passengers, fearing the worst, handed over their money and valuables.

Michael O'Connell wrote about Collier: *"He was reckless, generous and often gallant... He was born in 1789 and died of cholera in Drogheda in 1849...He was loved by the poor and even harboured by the not-so-poor when hard pressed...He is supposed to have avoided execution by escaping from jail in Trim and swimming the Boyne"* [41].

Santry was also prey to the heinous crime of grave robbing. Bodies were stolen from St. Pappan's graveyard. B.W. Adams said of a robber buried in 1829, he had: *"his body stolen and head removed for the sake of his teeth"* [42].

Further north the little village of Toberbunny was said by Adams (1883) to be known as: *"Robbers' Row from the lawless character of its inhabitant"* [43].

Living Conditions

Archer's Survey of 1801 tells of large farmers *"adequately housed"* [44], while small farmers had *"moderate accommodation"* [45]. This contrasted sharply with living conditions of the poor. They lived in thatched, mud walled cabins, which were expensive to maintain due to the high cost of thatch and were easily burned. The average labourer's wage, eight to nine shillings per week, remained static from 1801 to 1867.

The poor lived on a diet of potatoes and milk or occasionally had stirabout, made of oatmeal and water. Whiskey, rather than ale, was the preferred drink.

Morbiducci Pattern Shilling in Silver

Decrease in Crime

By the second half of the 19th century the area was more peaceful. Sir Charles Domville in an advertisement (in British newspapers, 1867) for farms to let in his Santry estate, described the area as: *"free from crime as shown in public records"* [46]. The mail coach era had passed and Santry had a police barracks on the site of today's *'Little Venice'* restaurant.

Farming

Samuel Lewis describing Santry (1837) wrote: *"the land is good quality, chiefly in meadow and pasture; that which is under tillage is fertile and the system of agriculture is improving"*[47].

Wheat, corn and vegetables were grown. Towards the end of the century dairy farming was widespread.

Rent, Cess and Tithe

Fears of increased rents discouraged farmers from improving their holdings. Rent on the Domville Estate in 1838 was three to four guineas per acre, increasing in 1867 to £6 to £7 per acre. Farmers also paid County Cess and County Tithe. Cess was based on rateable valuation and charged at two shillings per £1 of valuation.

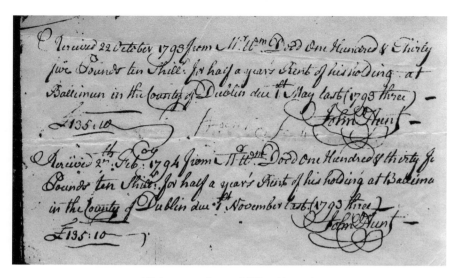

Picture courtesy of Olive Hegarty

Tithe Composition 1823

From 1823 onwards tithes were paid in money not in kind. A nationwide survey was carried out to determine how much each landholder should pay[48]. Tithe was based on the quality and price of wheat and oats. The Tithe Applotment Book for Santry shows rates ranging from 3s/4d to 3s/10d per acre.

Agricultural Depression

A long period of depression effecting both landlords and tenants began around 1870. By 1878 Sir Charles Domville was bankrupt. The land war, which began at this time, led to tenants buying their farms with financial help from the British Government. The era of the landlords was almost over.

The Domvilles 1810 - 1958

Sir Compton Domville (1810 - 1857)[49]

Sir Compton succeeded to Santry Estate in 1810 and gained a reputation as a hard working landlord. His first wife Elizabeth Lindsay, daughter of the Bishop of Kildare, died in childbirth in 1812. In 1815 he married Sarah Helena, daughter of Frederick Trench, Heywood, Queen's County. Sir Compton became Area Health Officer for County Dublin and was an M.P. for eighteen years.

Lady Sarah Helena was an artist whose drawings recorded the beauty of Santry Court.   She designed the Swiss Village built at Santry in 1840. In 1847 Sir Compton restored the Barry tomb in Santry Graveyard and provided a site for a Roman Catholic Church at Stormanstown.

He died in London in 1857 and was buried at Santry in a mausoleum erected by his son and heir Sir Charles Compton William. Lady Sarah Helena died in 1859 and was buried at Heywood mausoleum, Queen's County.

Sir Compton Domville mausoleum

Window dedicated to Lady Helena Domville

Sir Charles Compton William Domville (1857-1884)

Sir Charles was the most colourful of the Domvilles of Santry Court. He was artistic and temperamental. He planned every detail of the transformation of Santry Court and gardens in 1857. Stories of his escapades abound. According to one local tale he deserted the British Army during the Crimean War (1853-1856) and returned to Santry. His father, considering him a coward, banned him from Santry Court.

When his father died, Sir Charles, armed with pistols, stopped the funeral cortège from leaving the demesne. A hole had to be made in the wall to bring the coffin to Santry Church. Later, perhaps regretting his actions, he erected three memorials to his father at Santry Church.

In another incident, Sir Charles, in a rage, shot his favourite stallion El Abeiah. He later placed a monument to the horse in front of the mansion. Locals believed that the money earned by the stallion at stud, was buried under the monument. It fell, but no money was found.

In 1861 Sir Charles broke with tradition by marrying a Catholic, Lady Margaret St. Lawrence, daughter of the Earl of Howth. He converted to Catholicism. The contemporary press knew him as *"a distinguished convert"* [50] and *"a man of liberal instincts"* [51].

"Eleanor Cross" type pinnacle erected in memory of
Sir Charles' favourite stallion 'El Abeiah'.
Picture courtesy of Irish Architectural Archives

The Domville Medal

The couple held an annual prize-giving day[52]. Prizes were for craftwork, garden produce and stock. A Domville medal bearing the crests of all branches of the Domville family (designed by Sir Charles) was presented to his best tenants.

Sir Charles expected high standards from his workers. Labourers had to follow strict rules of dress and behaviour and be available at all times. They were instructed to have weekly baths in the farmyard washroom. No smoking was allowed near Santry Court in case of fire. Certain tenants were allowed only 1 month rent arrears instead of the usual 6 months, few evictions are recorded.

The restoration of Santry Court coupled with his lavish lifestyle led Sir Charles into financial difficulties. In 1878 he was declared bankrupt[53]. He left Santry with Lady Margaret to live in London. He died a broken man in 1884.

Lady Margaret turned her talents to writing and published *'A Life of Lamartine'* [54], a contemporary French mystic. She edited collected poems by Aubrey deVere. She died in 1929 and was buried with her husband at Southampton.

Sir Charles and Lady Margaret had no children. Sir Charles' brother, Sir William Compton succeeded him but died within two months. The estate then passed to Sir Charles' nephew, Sir Compton Meade Domville.

Domville Medal
Picture courtesy of Ken Finlay, Southside Newspapers

Sir Compton Meade Domville (1884-1935)[55]

When Sir Compton Meade succeeded to Santry estate it was already in decline. He had little interest in the property and lived mostly in London.

His sister, Mary Adelaide, married Sir William Hutchinson Poë of Ballinakill, Queen's County in 1886 and lived in Abbeyleix. Santry Court fell vacant. George Leslie Poë, captain of the Royal Navy and brother of Sir William H Poë, with his wife Mary Caldecott Poë and family moved into Santry Court in 1895. Mary died in 1924 and George in 1934. They are buried in the Domville plot in Santry.

Sir Compton Meade remained a bachelor. Older residents remember his funeral (1935). The coffin was taken to church on a horse-drawn farm cart decorated with ivy and flowers. Demesne workers and families followed the cortège.

Stained glass windows in St Pappan's church Santry

Sir Hugo Compton Domville Poë (1935-1958)

The next heir was Sir Hugo Compton Domville Poë, son of Mary Adelaide Domville and Sir William Hutchinson Poë. In order to inherit the estate, he had to assume the surname and arms of Domville. By an Act of Parliament (1936) he became Sir Hugo Compton Domville Poë Domville[56].
Sir Hugo was of unsound mind and lived in Portlaoise and took no part in the affairs of Santry estate. He died in 1958.

The Domville Curse

Local folklore tells of a curse on the Domville family, whereby no crow would build its nest and no lark would sing in the woods. When the last of the family died the crows and larks returned to Santry Woods.

Photograph of two of the drawing rooms in Santry Court
Photograph by James Simonton C1870 from "Lost Dublin" by Frederick O'Dwyer

Domville Dolls' House
With kind permission of the National Museum of Ireland

The house which was owned by the Domville family of Santry Court and Loughlinstown, Co Dublin was first exhibited in the Great Exhibition at the Crystal Palace, London, 1851. When the museum acquired the house in 1901 it was decided to have it furnished. The furniture was commissioned from the Cushendall toy industry, Co. Antrim, while the artist Mabel Hurst of Ranelagh, Dublin, painted the pictures, carpets and curtains.

The Twentieth Century - An Era of Change

The twentieth century was one of enormous change in Santry, when green fields gave way to housing and industrialisation. By the mid-twentieth century Santry Court was in ruins, its farm closed, its park and woodlands left unattended.

A taste of what lay ahead

In 1912 the first bi-plane seen here, landed in a field along Santry Avenue. While the captain dined with George Poë at Santry Court the plane was refuelled. A cart arrived with eight two-gallon cans of petrol, which was poured into the aircraft with a domestic funnel. It later took off in the direction of St. Pappin's Church, Ballymun. Schoolboy, Jack Duff, whose family farmed at Ballymun, recorded these events.

Within thirty years, Dublin Airport, only two miles away, was in operation and made its contribution to a changing Santry.

Development in public transport

Travel through Ballymun up to 1920 was by charabanc. On the Swords Road two private bus companies 'Irish General' and 'Garryowen' vied for business. In 1926 the Dublin United Tram Company introduced the '41' route to Swords through Santry[57]. The '64' route went to Portrane. Ballymun Road was served by the '60' to Lea's Cross and a twice weekly bus to Garristown. For many years, public transport facilities did not keep pace with the growing population, but have improved recently.

Charabanc
Picture courtesy of The National Transport Museum

No 60 Bus
Picture courtesy of The National Transport Museum

Santry - Cloghran - Swords bus
Picture courtesy of the National Transport Museum

Working Life

Farming dominated working life until the end of the 1930s. The Census of 1901 shows 58% of the population engaged in agriculture, of which 80% were farm labourers[58]. Many of the farms listed in 1901 were attached to big houses like Whitehouse, Santry Hall, Magenta Hall, Royal Oak and Santry Court. Farms were mainly owner-occupied with labourers living in rented houses nearby.

Magenta Hall

Royal Oak

White House Santry. Duff Family home from 1915 to 1947 approx.

Picture courtesy of Olive Hegarty

Changes in Farming

Rural electrification and mechanisation in the 1930s improved farming life but labourers had to find work elsewhere. Many were employed in the building and development of Dublin Airport, which began in 1936. Some emigrated and others worked in the new industries coming to Santry at that time.

Farming During the Emergency

Because of the food shortages during World War II, people were forced into self-sufficiency. Santry people grew vegetables in allotments that were along the Swords Road from Santry Village to Ellenfield Park. Local children worked thinning turnips for 6d per drill. At peak fruit picking time, Santry women spent long hours working on fruit farms as far away as Donabate.

The 1946 Harvest

Corn production increased during the war years because of compulsory tillage. When the 1946 crop faced ruin from bad weather, Taoiseach, Eamon de Valera, appealed to urban dwellers for help. In response, civil servants joined farmers in Santry to cut the corn with scythes. The harvest was saved. At one farm the civil servants were given a souvenir three-penny piece for their help.

The threepence

Decline in Farming

The encroachment of housing and industry from 1940s onwards made farming no longer viable. Land was sold for housing as early as 1930 when St. Canice's Terrace, Swords Road was built on part of Collins' farm. Twenty-six cottages were built at Turnapin in 1936. Sites along the Swords Road, part of Royal Oak Farm, were sold during the war years.

The first farm to completely disappear was *'Whitehouse'*. Its entrance is now Shanowen Road. Its orchard of 108 apple trees became the site of Buckley's Motor Car Assembly Plant. Whitehouse land and O'Dolan's land became the site for the Wates housing development of 1950.

1949 – Whitehouse –
Shanowen Road

Picture courtesy of Olive Hegarty

TELEPHONE NO. 44677.

34, Upper O'Connell Street.

Dublin, C6   7th June   19 47

Mrs. Mary E. Duff,

 Whitehouse,

  Santry, Co. Dublin.

To Kennedy & McGonagle, Solicitors, Dr.

YOU - to - WHITEHOUSE, LTD.

Lands Whitehouse, Santry.

Fee to cover all charges, exclusive of outlay, including preparation of Contract for sale of above lands at the sum of £18,000, preparation of all documents leading to Discharge of Equities, Discharging Equities, furnishing Title, obtaining and furnishing Certificate of discharge from Income Tax, correspondence and attendances re claim made by Mr. Kevin Duff, and correspondence and attendance on Mr. G. L. McGowan, Solicitor, re residence at Drishogue   250 0 0

OUTLAY:

Stamp on Contract			6
Commissioner's fees		4	0
Land Registry fees	8	16	0
Paid for Certificate of Valuation		8	6
Writing up Folio		1	0
Paid for Search		16	0
Paid for Certified Copy Will		6	0
Paid O'Hagan & Son re explaining Acts on Search	1	1	0
Commissioner's fees on 3 Declarations		6	0
Stamp Duty on 3 Declarations		7	6
Postages, parchment, stationery etc.	1	0	0
	13	4	3

250 0 0
13 4 3
£263 4 3

Solicitors.

Invoice courtesy of Kennedy & McGonagle, Solicitors & Olive Hegarty

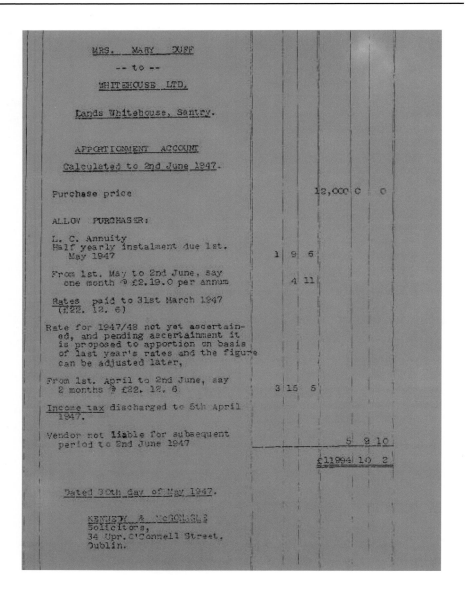

MRS. MARY DUFF

-- to --

WHITEHOUSE LTD,

Lands Whitehouse, Santry.

APPORTIONMENT ACCOUNT

Calculated to 2nd June 1947.

Purchase price				12,000	0	0
ALLOW PURCHASER:						
L. C. Annuity Half yearly instalment due 1st. May 1947	1	9	6			
From 1st. May to 2nd June, say one month @ £2.19.0 per annum	4	11				
Rates paid to 31st March 1947 (£22. 12. 6)						
Rate for 1947/48 not yet ascertained, and pending ascertainment it is proposed to apportion on basis of last year's rates and the figure can be adjusted later,						
From 1st. April to 2nd June, say 2 months @ £22. 12. 6	3	15	5			
Income tax discharged to 5th April 1947.						
Vendor not liable for subsequent period to 2nd June 1947				5	9	10
				£11994	10	2

Dated 30th day of May 1947.

KENNEDY & McGONAGLE
Solicitors,
34 Upr. O'Connell Street,
Dublin.

Invoice courtesy of Kennedy & McGonagle, Solicitors & Olive Hegarty

44

Santry Demesne Farm

Santry Demesne farm closed in 1948. Redundant workers were employed initially in preparation for the building of a sanatorium. When that project was abandoned, they worked for the Post Office and were housed in the new estate at Santry Villas, which was built on Domville land bought by Dublin County Council for £700.--.--

Travelling Salesmen

Among the characters who called regularly to Santry were: *"Badger"* who sold boots and shoes; *"Northlights"* who sold razors and blades, and older residents remember an Indian who sold ties and waistcoats. A clock salesman sold Westminster chiming clocks, costing thirty shillings, which could be paid for at 1/= (one shilling) per week.

Santry's 'Motown' Period

From 1949 to the early 1980s Santry had a thriving motor industry. Santry Garage at the corner of Coolock Lane, (now Fast Fit Exhausts), were sole agents for luxury Bristol cars, retailing in 1951 at £2,500.--.--

Buckley Motors (1949-1966), McCairns Motors (1957-1985) and Chrysler (Irl.) Ltd. (1972-1985) all assembled cars here. D.H.Sherrard (1958-1982), replacing Santry Garage, distributed agricultural machinery. J.H.Savilles, traders in Transport, Industrial and Agricultural Machinery, had their office and works in Santry Village (1949-1982) [59].

Santry's 'Motown' period is past

The Garda Station is now on the Buckley/Chrysler site, while Omni Park Shopping Centre was built on McCairns Motors' land in 1991.

Picture courtesy of Jim Cullen

47

THE BEST SMALL CAR
IN THE WORLD

he Simca has so many good
oints that, whatever your
articular requirements, you
now that the Simca is
be only practical answer!
Ask any Simca owner!

1959
MONTE CARLO RALLY
SIMCA
FIRST IN ITS CLASS
SECOND IN GENERAL
CLASSIFICATION

The famous " Flash " engine gives you terrific
power and speed with amazing economy.

The 4-speed gear-box has a smooth, positive
steering-column gear change.

There's space for five husky adults in the
roomy body.

The " Air France " seats are so comfortable,
especially on long journeys.

The huge boot holds all the luggage you'll
ever need.

The front suspension is designed to give per-
fect steering, safety and stability at any speeds.

*The Simca is the car with 14 world
records — 38 days and nights at 70
m.p.h. for 63,000 miles. Never before has ANY car been driven so
far at such a rate of speed*

Assemblers & Distributors : **McCAIRNS MOTORS LTD., DUBLIN**

Picture courtesy of Jim Cullen

Prices (inc. Heater and Duty). Engine Specification. Performance Factors. Weight. Gears. Acceleration (3rd or Inter. and Top Gears). Max. Speeds. Hill Climbing. Fuel Consumption. Brakes.

	Eire £	Swiss £	U.K. £	RAC Rating	No. Cyls	Cubic Capc.	Bore mm.	Stroke mm.	Comp. Ratio (to 1)	Gross BHP
Wolseley 15/60 ...	875	870	936	13.2	4	1489	73	88.9	8.3	55
Peugeot 403 ...	855	811	1099	15.9	4	1468	80	73	7	65
Vanguard Six ...	—	—	1022	24.1	6	1998	74.7	76	8	85
Ford Zodiac ...	885	1000	957	25.3	6	2553	82.6	79.5	7.8	90
Sunbeam Rapier	908	1050	986	15.4	4	1494	79	76.2	9.2	78
*Riley 4/68 ...	945	1025	1028	13.2	4	1489	73	88.9	8.3	66
Vauxhall Cresta	975	1020	1014	25.3	6	2651	82.5	82.5	8.1	113
Borg. Isabella ...	985	846	1198	13.9	4	1493	75	84.5	7	66
Borg. Isabella T.S.	1150	985	1375	13.9	4	1493	75	84.5	8.2	82
Austin A99 ...	1080	1280	1149	23.2	6	2912	83.3	88.9	8.2	112
Peugeot Diesel ...	1085	969	—	17.9	4	1816	85	80	21	55
Peugeot 404 ...	1095	880	1297	17.4	4	1618	84	73	7.2	72
Humber Hawk	1124	1160	1241	26.2	4	2267	81	110	7.5	78
Mercedes 180 ...	1160	1075	1694	17.9	4	1897	85	83.6	7	78
Super Snipe ...	1325	1500	1489	28.3	6	2965	87.3	82.5	8	129
Mercedes Diesel	1435	1208	1928	17.9	4	1897	85	83.6	21	55
Citroen ID19 ...	1450	986	1486	15	4	1911	78	100	7.5	66
Rover 100 ...	1575	—	1538	22.5	6	2625	77.8	92.1	7.8	104
Jaguar 2.4 ...	1598	1690	1534	25.6	6	2483	83	76.5	8	120
Jaguar 3.4 ...	1858	1960	1669	25.6	6	3442	83	106	8	210
Borgward 2.3 ...	1735	1450	2395	20.9	6	2240	75	84.5	8.2	100
Mercedes 220S ...	1795	1550	2524	23.8	6	2195	80	72.8	8.7	124
Rover 3 Litre ...	—	1600	1783	22.5	6	2995	77.8	105	8.75	115
Jaguar MK.IX ...	2085	2700	1884	28.1	6	3781	83	106	8	220
Alvis Saloon ...	2450	—	2823	26.2	6	2993	84	90	8.5	124
R-R Silver Cloud	5225	5084	6093	53.6	8	6230	104	91	8	Maker just says "Sufficient"!

	at RPM	BMEP lbs. psi	Max Tor. Lb/Ft	at RPM	Kerb Weight Cwt	Gears	MPH 0—50 Secs.	MPH 0—60 Secs.	MPH 0—70 Secs.	MPH 20—40 Secs.	MPH 30—50 Secs.
Wolseley 15/60 ...	4400	137	8[illegible]	2100	22	4	15.6	25.6	42.5	7.5	9.3
Peugeot 403 ...	4900	125	74	2500	21	4(o/d)	17	24.5	40.5	10	10
Vanguard Six ...	4500	133	107	2500	22¾	3	11.8	17	25.5	6.3	7.1
Ford Zodiac ...	4400	129	133	2000	23¼	3	11.5	19	22.5	5.6	6.5
Sunbeam Rapier	5400	137	83	3500	20¾	4(o/d)	11.7	16.5	23.2	3.3	3.7
*Riley 4/68 ...	5000	136	82	2500	22½	4	13	19	28	8	8.5
Vauxhall Cresta	4800	138	148	2400	23½	3	11	16	22	5.4	5.6
Borg. Isabella ...	4700	132	80	2400	20	4	15	23.5	37	8.2	9
Borg. Isabella T.S.	5200	140	83	3000	20	4	14	20	32	7.8	8.3
Austin A99 ...	4750	134	165	2500	30	3(o/d)	12.5	16	23.2	5.9	6.3
Peugeot Diesel ...	4000	—	68	2250	21½	4(o/d)	18	30	52	—	—
Peugeot 404 ...	5400	144	94	2250	20½	4(o/d)	14	20	28	8	8.9
Humber Hawk	4400	131	120	2300	28	4	14	20	30	7	8
Mercedes 180 ...	4500	141	100	2500	23½	4	13.5	20	30	7.5	9.5
Super Snipe ...	4800	135	162	1800	31	3	12	16.5	23	6.2	6.8
Mercedes Diesel	4000	108	83	2200	23½	4	18	26	44	9	11
Citroen ID19 ...	4500	126	98	2500	23	4(o/d)	15	20	29	10.4	10.9
Rover 100 ...	4750	130	138	1500	29	4(o/d)	12	17.5	27	7	7.2
Jaguar 2.4 ...	5750	142	144	2000	27½	4	9.9	14.4	22	5.3	4.8
Jaguar 3.4 ...	5500	155	215	3000	27¾	4(o/d)	7	9.1	12.4	5.3	4.8
Borgward 2.3 ...	5100	128	126	2800	26	4	10.8	14.6	20	6.5	7
Mercedes 220S ...	5200	138	139	3700	26	4	11.5	14.8	19	4.5	7.5
Rover 3 Litre ...	4500	136	164	1500	31½	4	11.7	16	22.7	6.3	6.7
Jaguar MK.IX ...	5500	157	240	3000	34½	4(o/d)	8.5	11.5	15	5.1	5.2
Alvis Saloon ...	4000	123	152	2500	31	4	9.3	13.5	18.3	6.2	6.7
R-R Silver Cloud	Maker just says "Sufficient"!				40½	Auto	8	11	15	4	5

	Standing ¼ mile Secs.	Top Gear MPH	3rd or inter MPH	Top Gear Max Gradient	mpg at steady speed 50 MPH m.p.g.	60 MPH m.p.g.	70 MPH m.p.g.	Disc Brakes	Fr... in.
Wolseley 15/60 ...	23.2	77	62	1 in 12	33	29	23	No	50
Peugeot 403 ...	21	81	75	1 in 24	36	31	26	No	50
Vanguard Six ...	21.3	73	46	1 in 11½	28	25	22	No	48
Ford Zodiac ...	20.5	90	60	1 in 8	26	24	21	Extra	53
Sunbeam Rapier	20.9	85	65	1 in 7½	32	29	24	Front	51
*Riley 4/68 ...	21.5	88	70	1 in 11	31	29	23	No	50
Vauxhall Cresta	20	94	60	1 in 9	29	25	22½	No	52
Borg. Isabella ...	22	80	60	1 in 12½	42	34	24	No	51
Borg. Isabella T.S.	21.5	90	70	1 in 12	38	32	22	No	51
Austin A99 ...	21	98	56	1 in 10	25	23	21	Front	53
Peugeot Diesel ...	24	73	55	—	48	38	30	No	50
Peugeot 404 ...	22.5	92	70	1 in 7	37	31	27	No	50
Humber Hawk	22	85	65	1 in 10	25	23	21	Front	54
Mercedes 180 ...	22	80	73	1 in 14½	35	31	26	No	50
Super Snipe ...	21	93	62	1 in 8	25.5	23	20	Front	54
Mercedes Diesel	—	70	50	1 in 17	50	44	32	No	50
Citroen ID19 ...	22.5	87	87	1 in 16	37	32	28	Front	49
Rover 100 ...	21	88	62	1 in 9	26	23	18	Front	49
Jaguar 2.4 ...	19.5	102	70	1 in 9	27	25	22	Yes	52
Jaguar 3.4 ...	17.2	120	97	1 in 7	28	25	23	Yes	52
Borgward 2.3 ...	20	95	86	1 in 9½	30	26	22	No	51
Mercedes 220S ...	19.5	102	75	1 in 9½	37	33	28	No	54
Rover 3 Litre ...	20.1	97	66	1 in 11	25	22	20	Front	53
Jaguar MK.IX ...	18	110	80	1 in 7	21	19	17	Yes	49
Alvis Saloon ...	19.5	95	83	1 in 9½	23½	22½	20½	Front	50
R-R Silver Cloud	18	112	70	1 in 7½	17½	17	15½	No	48

† Same as Wolseley 6/99 except for price and trim. * Same as Magnette (£925)

SUNBEAM RAPIER

GIVES YOU INDIVIDUALITY . . . .

Monte Carlo Rally 1961 ! The Sunbe[illegible] was 1st British car for the fourth ye[illegible] (irrespective of price, size or class

You must drive this latest 1½ litr[illegible] Rapier to see for yourself how it [illegible] standards for performance, safety, comfort and looks. £88[illegible]

Assembled by Buckley's Motors Ltd., Wh[illegible]

Picture courtesy of Jim Cullen

Infrastructural Change

As the transformation of Santry continued, many of the fine old houses gave their names to either housing or industrial estates. Road widening took with it old landmarks such as the Village Cottage on Santry Avenue and Santry Cottage on Coolock Lane corner.

- To ease traffic congestion through Santry to Dublin Airport and beyond, the M1 by-pass was opened in 1987.
- The Northern Cross Route passing through Ballystruan, Ballymun, Turnapin Great and Turnapin Little was opened in December 1996.
- Primary and post-primary schools were built in Ballymun. We got two new churches - Blessed Virgin Mary, Shangan (1976) and Blessed Margaret Ball, Santry (1994).
- Dardistown Cemetery with 250,000 burial plots opened in 1990.
- (A.L.S.A.A.) Aer Lingus Social and Athletic Association's pitch and putt course covers Tobberbunny townland.
- Despite local objections, plans to site the portals of Dublin Port Tunnel in Santry are going ahead.

Conclusion

As we approach the end of the twentieth century, the redevelopment of Santry demesne is beginning and introduces a new and interesting chapter in Santry's story.

Toll House - Village Cottage
Picture courtesy of Mena Cribben

Santry Today

Santry today is in a state of flux. All around we see, hear, smell, step over and drive around the evidence of immediate physical change to our area.

Work is progressing on the Port Tunnel south and east of the village and Omni Park Shopping Centre is a huge change from the group of shops that previously served the community. At the heart of Santry, where the former palatial home of the Domvilles stood, the development of Santry Woods is proceeding. There are five storey apartment blocks and a business park/office campus being constructed in Santry Demesne. Northward, the natural expansion of Dublin airport, means increased passing traffic, on land and in the air. Westward, there is a major housing development at Ballymun. To the East we look forward to the construction of a theme park and leisure complex.

Bombarded from all sides by the trappings of 'progress', we wonder if our village will ever be one whole unit again. We hope that the completion of the proposed public park, restoration of the temple, and development of a woodland and lake in the demesne, will provide a haven of tranquillity for locals, flora and fauna alike. We look forward to the time when all roadwork and developments have ceased and the last heavy machine has been withdrawn from the area. The best of the old and the new will be embraced. Residents will regroup and re-identify with their home and be proud of Santry at last.

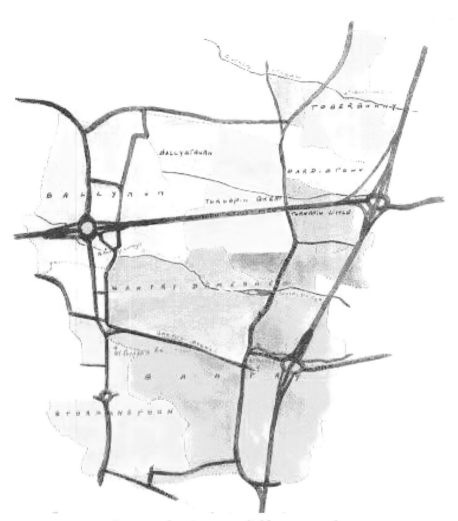

Santry today, its green fields eaten up by
shops, housing, industrial estates, and surrounded
and intersected by motorways

©Ordnance Survey Ireland/Government of Ireland.
Copyright Permit No. MP 000607

The Thatched Cottage

One of the oldest buildings in the area must be the thatched cottage in Dardistown. The earliest record of the house was circa 1600. The original house was extended in 1830 and 1840. There are nine rooms, including the hallway.

The original straw thatch roof rotted and the oak beams were eaten by woodworm. It was blown off in 1942. The walls were made of mud and wattle and mice had tunnelled through. The house was condemned when purchased by its present owner, Mr. George McCullough, Chief Executive of Dublin Cemetries. The tunnels were filled in with concrete and the thatched roof restored. It is now a protected structure. The pretty gardens surrounding it are protected also.

The house and the 1,500 acre farm belonged to the O'Donoghue family and was known as 'The Model Dairy Farm'. It was the precursor of Premier Dairies. The three deep artesian wells on the property made this possible.

The Thatched Cottage at Dardistown

Gable end Thatched Cottage at Dardistown
Pictures courtesy of George McCullough

Gates at Dardistown Cemetry[60]

The gates now at Dardistown were manufactured in 1840. They came from the old St. Paul's section, Glasnevin Cemetery. They were on a scrap heap until they were restored in 1989 and erected at Dardistown Cemetry in 1990.

Gates at Dardistown Cemetery
Picture courtesy of Ismail Dadabhay

Santry Court and Demesne

The Beginning of Santry Demesne

Santry Court is first recorded in the Civil Survey of 1654 as *"a dwelling house of stone, with a barne and old stable, thatch ye walls of a house and garden and two orchards, and six acres of ashgrove"* [61]. From these origins evolved one of the finest houses and gardens in County Dublin.

Santry Court & Demesne from a Pen & Ink Estate Map, 1812

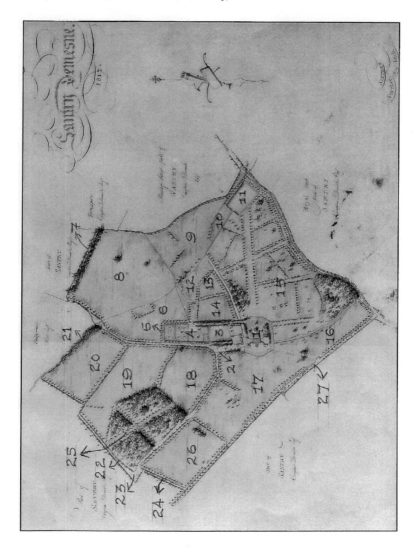

Source: Ms. NLI., Ms. 16. F. 4 (1). Domville Estate Maps, 1812.

Courtesy of the National Library of Ireland

Key to map[62]

1.	Mansion, out-offices and shrubbery	**15.**	Plantation, widening back avenue
2.	Approach	**16.**	Lawn
3.	Pigeon Park and Plantation	**17.**	Front Lawn
4.	Gardens	**18.**	Horse Pasture
5.	Plantation	**19.**	Loughlargon
6.	Pasture	**20.**	Coleman's Park Meadow
7.	Firgrove	**21.**	Grove
8.	Bullockhill	**22.**	Old Road/Avenue
9.	Pasture	**23.**	Do
10.	Pasture	**24.**	Do
11.	Pond	**25.**	Wood
12.	Pasture	**26.**	Wenches Meadow
13.	Pasture	**27.**	Santry Ave-Entrance off Santry Ave
14.	Pasture		

Santry Court

Henry Barry, third Lord Santry built a Queen Anne style mansion in 1702. Samuel Lewis (1837) described it as *"a stately mansion of brick, containing many spacious apartments, ornamented with numerous family portraits, a valuable collection of historical and scriptural paintings by the best masters and many items of fine arts"* [63].

According to Lewis the demesne covered *"140 acres laid out in pleasure grounds, richly embellished with trees"* [64].

The access avenue from the *"grand gates"* on the Swords Road was lined with Walnut trees and American Cedars. North of the house, there were walled fruit gardens, extensive greenhouses and the farmyard.

Picture courtesy of the National Library of Ireland

Life at Santry Court

The family entertained lavishly. Eight hundred guests attended a ball in 1860[65]. Fifty-two maids lived in the house. Labourers and their families lived in lodges throughout the demesne. The 'lodgers' owned only their bedclothes and were moved at the whim of the landlord. 'Oakdale' (formerly Oak Lodge) on Santry Avenue, still survives. (Picture below)

Picture courtesy of Joseph & Olivia Morgan

Restoration of House and Gardens

Sir Charles restored the house, gardens and out-offices in 1857. All 130 apartments were elaborately re-decorated. Some windows were replaced with stained glass and a water supply was laid on to the house from the river.

There was a rose garden added to the redesigned gardens. Ornamental gas lamps lit the avenue and a replica Phoenix monument was placed in the grounds. In the farmyard the dairy walls were lined with china plates.

The temple, built at Templeogue in 1748 by Sir Compton Domville was re-erected at Santry. Rows of beech trees were planted leading to it. The restoration cost £45,987.0.0[66], Sir Charles thought that he had created an everlasting monument to the name Domville in County Dublin.

Phoenix monument
Picture courtesy of Irish Architectural Archives

The Temple Santry Demesne
Picture courtesy of Irish Architectural Archives

End of a Dream

The dream was short-lived. Twenty years later he was declared bankrupt. Almost the entire contents of Santry Court were sold to cover his debts. By the 20th century the estate was depleted. The income from tenants rent was almost gone. The farm was no longer viable and was closed in 1948.

62

The Fall of Santry Court

Grangegorman Mental Hospital Board bought the property in 1939 for £17,000. Soldiers were billeted there during the war. A fire on the night of 24th October 1941 left the house in ruins[67]. Plans to use the site for sheltered accommodation were dropped and preparations to build a sanatorium were also abandoned. The house lay derelict until its demolition in 1959.

Close up view of door case in Santry Court
Pictures courtesy of Irish Architectural Archives

Demesne Folklore

Helen, a maid from Santry Court, walked regularly by night on a tree-lined path that ran through the demesne. She was murdered there. Her ghost was said to appear along the path known as *"Helen's Walk"*.

Demolition of Santry Court 9th April 1959
Picture courtesy of the late Peter Fowler

New Owners

Billy Morton built Santry Sports Stadium on part of the demesne in 1958 and Trinity College opened their sports grounds and library archives on a site along Santry Avenue. The remainder was privately owned.

Since the 1950s the demesne has suffered from natural deterioration and vandalism. The issue of conservation was raised. Santry Community Association and other Residents' Groups have been to the fore in efforts to have the estate developed as a public amenity. Their efforts have been rewarded in the proposed development plan.

Picture of Billy Morton by kind permission of the Morton Family

St Pappan's Church and Graveyard

St. Pappan's Church and graveyard are a historical microcosm of Santry. There has been a church on this site since earliest Christian times.

The present St. Pappan's (1709) replaced an early 13th century church built by Anglo-Norman invader Adam de Phoepe.

Mortuary Urn to Sir Compton Domville

Graveyard

Richard and Henry Barry second and third Lords of Santry are buried here. The Domville plot contains the tombs of Sir Compton (d.1857) and Sir Compton Meade (d.1935). Other Domvilles of Santry Court are buried throughout the graveyard alongside the people of Santry, Protestant and Catholic who were buried here through the centuries.

67

Memorials

Inside the church there are many memorials to the families who lived in Santry Court. The cover of the Barry tomb hangs on the south wall. Made of brass, it is dedicated to *'Richard Baron of Santry and his Lady'* [68]. It is one of only two such memorial brasses in Ireland.

Richard and Henry Barry are recalled on two marble plaques[69]. Among the Domvilles commemorated are Sir Charles Polkington and Lady Margaret who inherited Santry estate in 1768 and Sir Compton and his first wife Elizabeth who died in 1812[70].

St Pappan's Church organ (Benson) Circa 1900

Stained Glass Windows

Three of the stained glass windows are dedicated to the Poë family, George and Mary and Charles Vernon who died in the Great War. The fourth window commemorates Lady Helena Domville of Swiss Village fame.

Stained glass windows in St Pappan's church
Top window is *Phoebe* by Hubert Mc Goldrick[71]
Left window is *Justice & Fortitude* by Catherine O'Brien
Right window is *Michael the Archangel* by Hubert Mc Goldrick

The Baptismal Font [72]

The 16th century font stands to the right of the entrance. Hexagonal in shape and made of Yorkshire stone, it has marks on the top said to have been made by Charles Coote's soldiers sharpening their swords before the Battle of Santry (1641).

Rev. B.W. Adams, a Santry historian, recovered the font from the local forge, where it was being used to store water for cooling horseshoes. He placed it in its present position in 1877.

Glebe House[73]

Picture courtesy of Ernest Barrett

The Glebe House (1829) stands behind the graveyard. Recently a parish hall was built on glebe land adjoining the Church. This hall is available for use by the wider community.

Tower House - Santry Charter School

Tower House (1708) was originally a mill. In 1744 the Incorporated Society for the Promotion of Protestant Schools in Ireland founded Santry Charter School there[74]. This school was one of many founded by Royal Charter of 1733 to instruct poor Catholic children in the Protestant religion. R. H. L. Gardner gave 31 acres of land to Santry school and Primate Boulter of Dublin donated £400.

Sixty girls, aged 5-13 years lived there. It was later extended to accommodate 150 pupils. The girls were taught the 3 Rs, spinning and weaving. They worked on the school farm. The local vicar gave weekly religious instruction.

Tower House, Ballymun Cross
Picture courtesy of Pat York

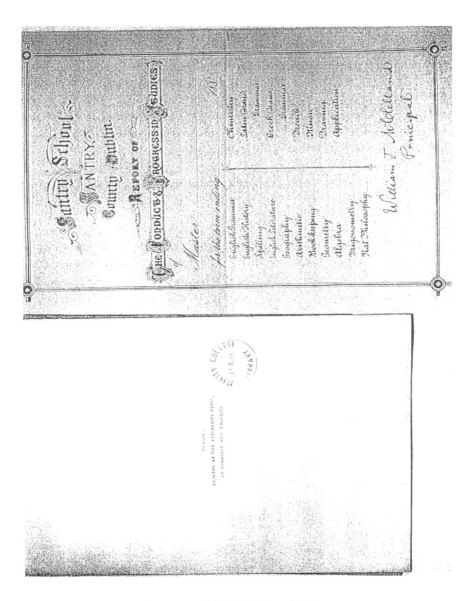

Courtesy of Trinity College Dublin

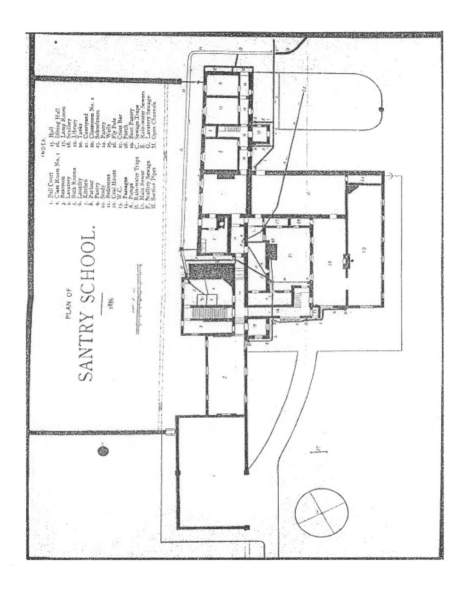

Courtesy of Trinity College Dublin

Ballymun Villa – Headmasters' House
Picture courtesy of Olive Hegarty

Miserable Objects

Initially the system worked well. However, in a damning report in 1825 it was stated *"the children of Santry school were sickly and pale and such miserable objects that they were a disgrace to all society. Their reading had been neglected to make them work for their masters"* 75. Government funding was withdrawn bringing an end to the Charter School system by 1830.

Highly Commended

The school became a thriving middle-class school for boys, under the Incorporated Society, run by headmasters and known as a Technical, Scientific and Commercial Institution. W. J. McClelland, headmaster in the 1880s was highly commended by A. S.

75

Hart, Vice Provost of Trinity College, for the way in which the school was run[76]. The prospectus shows that a wide range of subjects was taught, with provision for music, sport and bible study. Pupils were prepared for work in the civil service and banks and for entry to all colleges, where they were high achievers. In 1895 the property reverted to private ownership.

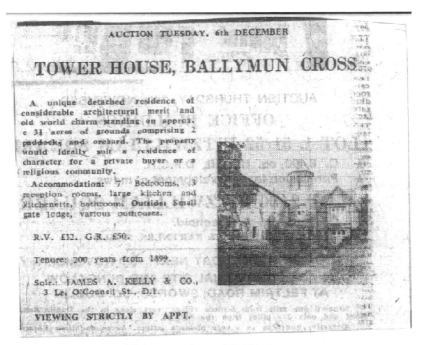

Picture courtesy of Pat York

I.R.A. H.Q.

In the 1920s Tower House became the Dublin headquarters of the old I.R.A. A secret cupboard in an upstairs bedroom could accommodate two people. Frank Aiken T.D. admitted being a *'guest'* in this cupboard which remained undiscovered through many intensive searches.

On the 1972 Development Plan for the area, Tower House was designated for possible preservation. Unfortunately it was destroyed by fire, caused by vandals, in the early 1980s.

The Jackson School

In 1756, John Jackson, vicar of Santry, set up a school in the village for Protestant children[77]. The 1st schoolmaster's pay was a princely £6 annually. It became known as the Jackson School and was part of the National School system before its closure in 1925. The teacher's house was used as a family home until recently. Schoolhouse Lane, Santry Village, takes its name from the Jackson School.

The Jackson family were friends of Dean Jonathan Swift. The Dean remembered them in his will, bequeathing to them, according to Dalton *"his horses and horse furniture and third best beaver hat"* [78].

Picture courtesy of Sheila Field

The Jackson Plaque

*This School House was Built in the pursuance
of the Will of the Rev[d] Daniel Jackson of
Clonshagh formerly Vicar of Santry who left
a considerable part of a moderate Fortune
for the support thereof.
This Building was begun & finish'd by the
Rev[d] John Jackson of Clonshagh Grandson
to the said Testator A.D. 1756.
The Gratefull Parishioners have caused this
Stone to be fix'd here in remembrance of
their Charitable worthy Benefactor.*

This plaque survives and can be seen at Schoolhouse Lane, Santry Village.

Swiss Village

Santry's Swiss Village was designed by Lady Sarah Helena Domville in 1840. It consisted of six neat cottages in Schoolhouse Lane and eleven semi-detached houses along the Swords Road[79]. The buildings along the Swords Road included a Forge, a Provision Store, a Post Office and Swiss style cottages. The cottages were named Rose, Verbena, Hawthorn, Jasmine, Chestnut and Woodbine and had tiny front gardens maintained by the demesne gardener.

The village cottage, Santry Avenue, a toll-house up to 1788, had its roof replaced to match the village houses[80].

The 1901 census shows Englishman Henry Harris owned the Swiss Village including Rose Cottage Public House. The forge remained with the Domvilles. Harris's property passed to his daughter Mrs. Clarke in 1915 and remained with the Clarkes until 1945.

Picture courtesy of Irish Architectural Archives

Rose Cottage Pub

The pub had a mud floor covered with sawdust and was lit by four brass lamps. The patrons were mainly farmers, as were the Clarkes, the proprietors. They kept cattle, sheep and pigs and also sold milk. The field opposite the village was called *'Clarke's eleven acre field.' (formerly Turnpike Field).*

Life in the Swiss Village

People were poor and lived simply. Rush carters going to Dublin market often dropped a bag of vegetables in the village. Children collected firewood while playing in Santry demesne. Water was carried from the village pump. After rural electrification the village had two lights that shone, it is said, mainly in the daytime.

Sport and Entertainment

Mummers from Swords and St. Margarets visited Santry in Winter. Dressed in colourful traditional costumes, they staged their drama, music and rhymes opposite the forge. Greyhound racing and later motorcycle racing were held in Clarke's field. In the 1940s Santry had a football team "Santry United." The team and supporters travelled as far as Balbriggan for matches, a long journey in those days.

Swords Mummers
Picture courtesy of Swords Heritage Group

Soccer Star

Kevin Clarke played for Drumcondra before turning professional. He played for Swansea Town and Preston Northend and was capped for Ireland in the late 1940s.

81

Pages from Rent Book for Jasmine Cottage

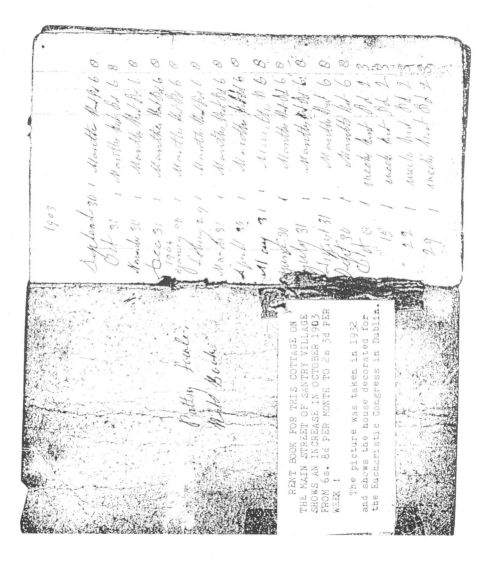

Picture courtesy of the late Peter Fowler

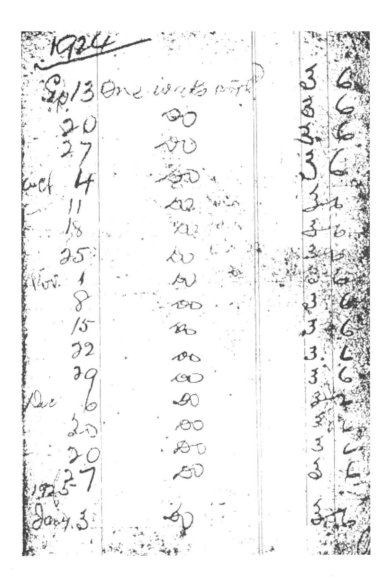

Picture courtesy of the late Peter Fowler

Customs and Folklore

On New Year's Eve, to announce the New Year, a local boy was pushed around in a handcart ringing a bell. Locals believed that a ghost haunted a byre near the village - even the cows were afraid until a priest laid it to rest in a nearby rockery.

The Forge

The building, with its horseshoe shaped doorway, stood opposite the end of Santry Avenue. It was run by the Madden family, master blacksmiths, for almost 90 years. Michael Madden came to Santry with Lady Margaret St. Lawrence when she married Sir Charles Domville in 1861. The Maddens shod horses, repaired farm machinery, made gates and 'shod' carts for farmers and carriers. During frosty weather special nails were put in the horseshoes to help the horses pull uphill. When they were busy, journeymen blacksmiths were employed.

By 1951 "planes from the nearby airport cast shadows across the old village street and across the lives of its inhabitants" [81]. Michael Madden descendant of the former master blacksmith knew that his time as village blacksmith was over. "Quietly he closed the doors of the old forge and next day was gone" – another man gone from the village – emigrated [82].

The Forge Santry
Picture courtesy of
Swords Heritage Group

Mary Murphy (R.I.P.)
Daugher of Michael Madden
one of the village blacksmiths

Changes[83]

In 1945 the Belton Group bought Clarke's property in the village. Jack Belton ran the pub until 1950. Eugene O'Reilly was publican from 1950 to 1972.

Cottages in Schoolhouse Lane were demolished in 1948. Families were re-housed in a new Council estate, Santry Villas.

The Gardai who came to the village in 1950 moved to Shanowen Road in 1985. T.O'Reilly, electrical suppliers, bought the barracks and recently replaced the building with a more modern one.

Ashleigh House, a grocery store from 1935 to 1970s, now houses offices, a hairdresser's shop and Mr. Perri's 'Take Away'.

J.H.Saville & Co. ran their business in 'Clarke's Field' 1949 to 1982. They sold a site to the Provincial Bank (now A.I.B.) in 1955. An office block and builders' providers now occupy Saville's site.

The Swiss Cottages gradually disappeared. Families were housed in Magenta Crescent estate built in 1966.

Verbena, the last Swiss Cottage, knocked in 1974 was replaced by an office building, featuring the original Swiss style gable. Our only reminder of the Swiss Village is in the name of the pub "The Swiss Cottage." It has been owned by Molloys since 1972.

Verbena the last Swiss Cottage
Picture courtesy of Independent Newspapers

Santry Village Post Office

Picture courtesy of Irish Architectural Archives

St. Pappin's Church and School - Ballymun

A Roman Catholic Church opened at Stormanstown in 1848, replacing Balcurris Church built in 1776 [84]. Although built in Stormanstown, this church became known as St. Pappin's, Ballymun. It was built on Domville land, given rent free by Sir Compton Domville, on condition that there would be no burials there. Other benefactors were James Coughlan, proprietor of the *'Cat and Cage'* public house Drumcondra and Paddy Delaney, blacksmith, who contributed £800 towards the Curate's house [85].

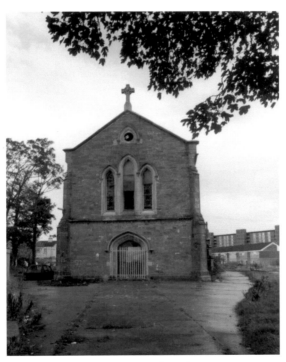

St Pappin's Church

Domville House Ballymun - Curates' House

Coachman

Tradition tells us that Sir Charles Domville's coachman, James Kelly, died as a result of a prank. Sir Charles gave permission to bury him at St. Pappin's. Later he accused Kelly's friends of breaking the terms of the lease and thereafter charged rent for the site.

Part of many Parishes[86]

As the Dublin Diocese developed St. Pappin's Church was part of Clontarf & Coolock (1848), Fairview (1879), Glasnevin (1912) and Larkhill (1944). The curate lived in the area.

Closure

St. Pappin's Church closed in 1982 following the building of a larger Church, Blessed Virgin Mary, Shangan (1976). Plans are now afoot to turn it into a nursing home.
*[St Pappin's - this spelling was used to differentiate between the church in Ballymun and the Church in Santry]

St. Pappin's School

A one-teacher school was built beside St. Pappin's Church c1864. It replaced Balcurris School and was called Ballymun National School.
In 1907 it became a two-teacher school and changed its name to St. Pappin's National School, Ballymun. An inspector's report of 1907 said: *"the school was suitably furnished and provided with musical instruments and typewriters"* [87].

School Orchestra

In the 1950s, St. Pappin's, then a three-teacher school, was noted for its orchestra which competed successfully at Feis Ceoil and other competitions throughout Ireland.

St Pappin's School Orchestra (circa 1958)
Photograph courtesy of Marie Ryan

Closure

The increase in population in Ballymun (1960s) led to the building of a larger school - Our Lady of Victories on Ballymun Road. St. Pappin's closed in 1965, the building is home to St. Pappin's Youth Club.

Mrs Kathleen Mulhall, celebrating her 91st birthday in her home in Coolock Lane, Santry. One of St. Pappin's much loved teachers, Kathleen is now in her 100th year. (Mrs Mulhall died in 2004) Photograph courtesy of Mulhall Family

Land League Cottages

During the land war, Charles Stuart Parnell authorised the building of cottages to house people living in poor conditions. Two of these cottages, built about 1870, stand at the corner of Santry Avenue and Ballymun Road. Each cottage had an acre of land for growing vegetables and fruit.

Our local postmistress Bean Ui Chribbín's grandparents, McCormacks, ran a small shop in one of the cottages. Supplies were brought from Phibsboro by donkey and cart. Lollipops, a farthing each, were sold to the boys from Santry School.
The cottages are due for demolition as part of *'Ballymun Regeneration'*.

The farthing (quarter of a penny)

Land League Cottages

*Bean Uí Chribbín's grandparents
(Paddy and Mary Anne Mc Cormack)
Photograph courtesy of Bean Uí Chribbín*

Santry Stadium

Clonliffe Harriers were founded in 1886 near Croke Park and moved to Santry Court in 1955, when the plan to build a TB Sanatorium was abandoned by Grangegorman Mental Health Board. Trees were felled to develop the stadium. It was said that Billy Morton (the driving force behind the stadium and the Irish National Marathon Champion 1936) *"would have no luck because he had upset the fairies"*. Locals believed that there were fairy forts in the woods.

Making Tracks

Billy Morton held a *"Sporting Press Conference"*. He said: "Grass is on the way out" and so the first modern cinder track in Ireland opened in 1958[88]. The terrace and cinder tennis courts were also built.

Herb Elliott ran the mile race here in a world record breaking time of 3 mins. 54 seconds (Aug. 6th 1958). For the first time in history the first five runners in the race broke the 4-minute mile barrier. It was thought the *"oxygen from the trees helped"*.

The stadium was called the JFK Stadium and later named Morton Stadium. The recession, at its hardest throughout the 80s, left the stadium in financial difficulties. Some trustees sold minerals to make money. Billy Morton paid groundsmen from his own pocket. Dickie Rock gave a benefit concert in the Olympia Theatre to a packed audience. Stockcar racing was run and part of the stadium was let for storage. There was no government support.

Public Ownership

In 1981 Jim Tunney was appointed Junior Minister for Sport. He set about replacing the cinder track with a polyurethane track and ownership was transferred to the state.

In 1993 the track was replaced, the club received other supports before the legal transfer was finally in place. It was opened by An Taoiseach, Bertie Ahern in 1995.

Once more renamed **Morton Stadium**, developments include indoor facilities i.e. an 86 metre track, high jump, long jump, pole vault and a gymnasium. There is an 800 seater covered stand and room for 18,000 spectators on the terraces. Facilities are available for Schools, Community, Sports, Youth and Fitness Groups. Morton Stadium was the athletic venue for the 2003 world Special Olympics. A new 200 metre indoor track and other facilities are planned. Morton Stadium will provide Irish Athletics with outdoor and indoor facilities in one venue.

Formal opening of Guinness cycle track in Santry. Cutting the tape
Mr Jackson of Guinness. Picture includes Billy Morton, President of
Clonliffe Harriers and Charlie Rothwell, Vice-President.
(Courtesy of Morton Family)

THE JOHN F. KENNEDY STADIUM

Before the erection of the new Grand Stand.

Ballymun

A section of Ballymun housing estate lies in the Santry area, situated to the east of the northbound dual carriageway, which divides the estate.

Originally it had been planned to develop Ballymun as a mixed class dormitory suburb of Dublin, however, because of a critical housing shortage, a scheme dedicated solely to high density social housing was built instead. This took the form of high rise building popular in Europe at the time.

In the Santry area terraced housing, four and eight storey blocks and three fifteen storey tower blocks were built. The tower blocks were named after signatories to the Proclamation of the Irish Republic, Sean McDermott, Thomas McDonagh and Padraig Pearse.

By completion in 1969, costing £10,000,000 — 3,021[89] housing sites had been built. New residents were delighted with the standard of their accommodation, but felt isolated - having been moved away from the support of extended family. Initially there were no basic community facilities such as shops provided. This made life very difficult.

There followed a period of unrest. The residents campaigned for the provision of essential services. One tool used in this campaign was 'rent strikes.'

Through the years of economic hardship Ballymun suffered many social problems. There has been a great community drive to solve these problems and as a result, a regeneration plan was agreed in 1998. This regeneration is expected to take 10 years to complete. The high rise concept in Ballymun will be consigned to history.

Top picture shows Coultry Road flats
Bottom picture shows Sean Mc Dermott flats

Chapel of Blessed Margaret Ball

This chapel, built at Oakpark in 1994, is dedicated to Blessed Margaret Ball, a sixteenth century Dublin martyr.

Margaret's son, Walter, a committed Protestant, was Mayor of Dublin 1580-1581[90]. He condemned his mother to prison where she died in 1584[91]. Walter's wife, Eleanor, was daughter of Alderman Robert Ussher of Santry, whose family leased lands here up to the mid-seventeenth century.

Local Wells

St. **Pappan's Well** is situated in a garden behind Ashleigh House, Santry Village. It is regarded locally as a holy well from St. Pappan's time. No devotions are held there now and it is overgrown.

Toberbunny Well

The townland of Toberbunny takes its name from this well, *'Tobar Bainne'* or *'Well of the milk'*[92]. It is situated close to the Cuckoo Stream, East-South-East of Toberbunny Bridge, on A.L.S.A.A. land.

In 1772 Dr. John Rutty analysed the water in Toberbunny Well and found it contained a small amount of alkaline salt, calcareous matter and some sulphur[93]. The well was never venerated but people believed in its curative powers and it was used during the Famine.

On a recent field trip in the area we found the well completely overgrown.

Toberbunny Bridge

Picture shows Cuckoo Stream

FLORA and FAUNA

The Flora and Fauna of Santry is not typical of a Dublin suburb. The presence of Santry Demesne covering many acres of the area has made a significant difference to evolution of the site as a habitat for flora and fauna.
The area lies 204' above sea level.

Santry Oaks

On a field trip through Santry Demesne members of Santry Guild were impressed by the variety of trees. Native trees exist alongside 'Exotics' thanks to Lady Helena. Beautiful old Oak trees grow in the demesne. A carved stone plaque has been found, it reads: *"The seed of these Evergreen Oaks was brought from Italy by Helena Lady Domville in 1840"*.
On other trees were oak apples (they are formed by wasps when nesting).

Top picture shows a Copper Beech tree in Geraldstown House
Bottom picture shows an Evergreen Oak tree in Santry Woods

Top picture shows Achillea
Bottom picture shows Wild Turnip

Cherry Blossom trees in Santry Close

Bats about Santry

Bat boxes hang on mature trees. Enquiries made to Bat Conservation Group informed us that (1) Leislers, (2) Pipistrelle 45KH2, (3) Pipistrelle 55 KH2 and (4)Brown long-eared bats, all live in the neighbourhood.

D.Nash '02

"Save Santry Woods"

Santry Woods was almost lost to North Dublin. Planning permission for development of the site was sought. Because of objections by local groups, who fought to have the area preserved as a natural treasure, an environmental impact study was undertaken[94]. The findings, (a matter of public record), show that in areas such as Black Wood, Fairy Grove and Old Forge, large tree loss means microclimate of shade and shelter no longer exists to support woodland plant and animal communities. There was much work to be done to save the woods.

New proposals were submitted and passed. They included a five-acre man-made lake to be restored to its former splendour in the centre of a seventy-five acre public park. An arboretum is also planned. This linear park, stretching from Old Ballymun Road through Temple Gardens to Swords Road, will go some way towards restoring the neglected parklands. In the commissioned survey, selective replanting is recommended. Many mature trees were thought worthy of preservation.

Picture courtesy of Ken Finlay, Southside Newspapers

Log pile from Santry Woods

Lakeside

The lake, now being restored, was never a natural lake. It was artificial and highly unusual. The landscaped area around the ornamental 'pond' boasted having several Yew trees, some located on the island in the centre of the lake. Adjacent to the pond is a row of planted Tilia trees - some of which have been granted Tree Preservation Orders (denoted by a metal tag attached to the trunk). Nesting in the area are Moorhens, Mallards, Herons, Passerines and Black Cap. A Kestrel was spotted in the Demesne during a field trip. The roosting site was identified as a large old pine tree. Droppings and castings (regurgitated fur balls), were found around the base of the tree. Grey squirrels abound throughout the site. The Santry River feeds the lake. It rises in Harristown, flows through the Stardust Memorial Park and enters the sea at North Bull Island. The park in Santry follows part of the path of the river.

Top picture shows a bridge in Santry Woods
Bottom picture shows the Lake in Santry Woods

Legally Protected Species

The evaluation stated: *"The value of the habitat is largely its rarity in North Dublin…it supports some characteristic flora and fauna"* [95].

"The remaining woods are of generally good quality and include Horse Chestnut, Beech, Wych Elm, Ash, Sycamore, Hawthorn, Birch, Alder, Scot's Pine and Oak. A wide range of herbaceous species was recorded including Wood Speedwell, Dog-violet, Goldilocks Buttercup and False Brome" [96].

A species, legally protected under the Flora Protection Order 1987, 'Hairy St. John's Wort', grows here. This riverbank perennial has been recorded from only five counties in eastern Ireland, concentrated in the River Liffey valley.

Another legally protected plant growing here is the *'Viola Hirta'*.

The work of restoration and selective preservation has commenced. Enquiries were made to 'Sap Nurseries' (commissioned to undertake the work).

15 each of Tilia europaea, Prunus avium, Acer platanoides and Crataegus monogyna were budded last summer. The balance of the plants will be grafted this season.

Wild Garlic in Santry Woods

107

Top picture shows Hypericum hirsutum L. (hairy St. John's wort)
Bottom picture shows Viola hirta L. (hairy violet)

A Neighbourhood Divided

Fingal Co. Council has responsibility for the land north of Santry Avenue/Coolock Lane while Dublin City Council has care of the area to the south.

Residents do a great service for their community in keeping neighbourhoods tidy, gardens beautiful and a watchful eye out for vandalism.

The last little hedgehog that lived in Santry Close was fed and welcomed by neighbours. Birds are fed in winter and bird-table watches have resulted in formidable lists of wild-bird names being kept. One such list counts Magpie, Thrush, Pigeon, Collared Dove, Wren, Robin, Blackbird, Blackcap, Starling, Crow, Wagtail, Siskin, Chaffinch, Goldfinch, Greenfinch, Bluetit, Coal Tit, Great Tit and Rooks among its visitors. A speckled wood Butterfly was spotted during the field trip in the Demesne.

Outstanding Specimens

Besides the Demesne there are many relatively new treasures worthy of mention. One outstanding feature is Santry Garda Station garden. It has two ponds and is very well maintained. Urban children can be seen frog-spawn hunting there.

Great specimen trees, such as the 150yr old Chestnut on the corner of Swords Road/Church Lane, the winter flowering Cherry tree outside Buckley's Hardware, Sycamore trees in the Graveyard, mature trees in the grounds of Geraldstown House (one flowering every month of the year) provide habitats for wildlife.

Chestnut tree on the corner of Swords Road/Church Lane

Santry Garda Station Garden and Pond

Survivors

The real heroes in the struggle for survival are the little wild creatures that, in spite of human neglect or interference, survive and continue to raise their young.   Progress can mean the destruction of habitats and feeding/breeding grounds of wild creatures. A caring and vigilant population will ensure their protection in Santry.

Place Names

Ballymun	1355	Baile Muine - Town of the Shrubbery.
Ballystruan	1415	Ballystrowan – Baile an tStrutháin. Town of the Stream.
Commons also called **Betty's Field**	1641 1812	An area in common ownership for grazing of animals.
Gibbet Park **Part of Commons**	1874	Marked on a map of Santry area. A place where people were hanged and their bodies left on display.
Dardistown	1415	Dardyestown – Townland of Dardis. An Anglo–Irish surname.
Santry **Seantrabh**	827	Seantrabh - Old Tribe. This tribe may have been the Almanii who according to The Book of Lechan lived here in pre-Celtic times.
Stormanstown	1419	Sturmynestown - Townland of Storman. An English surname possibly of Viking origin.
Toberbunny	1399	Tobar Bainne. Well of the milk so called from the whiteness of its water.
Turnapin Great and **Turnapin Little**	1837	Originally Penny Come Quick. May have referred to a turnstile.

Other Local Place Names

Magenta	Named after Magenta in Italy where Marshall McMahon and the French under Napoleon III overcame the Austrians on 4th June 1859. Marshall McMahon, who was Irish was made Duke of Magenta.
Turnpike Field	1700 – Swords Road opposite Santry Village. Named after the toll road now known as Santry Ave. Later it became Clarke's field where flapper greyhound meetings were held in the 1940s.
Furry Park	Part of Turnapin Great. Got its name from a type of furze bush growing there in the 1800s. George Egan M.P. lived there in 1800. He refused Baronetcy and £3,000 p.a. to support the Union of Britain and Ireland in 1801.

O.S. 14 Dublin   Surveryed in 1837   Revised in 1938
©Ordnance Survey Ireland/Government of Ireland.
Copyright Permit No. MP 000607

Family Names

*2 *3 Clarke	Descendant of Cléireach 820 AD. Originally from Galway. Settled in Ulster and the name anglicised to Clarke after the Ulster plantation of 1609.
*2 *3 Collins – Ó Coileáin	Either Irish or English origin. In Ireland it is an anglicisation of Ó Coileáin. Originally based in Limerick and dispersed to Cork after the Anglo-Norman invasion.
*2 Coughlan – Coghlan	Anglicised form of old Irish name Ó Cochláin. Diminutive of word for cape or hood. Two distinct septs, one in Cork and one in Offaly.
*1 Devine – Davin – Devane – Devins – Downes	Widespread Irish surname with diversity of spellings.
*2 Donohoe – Donohue – Donoghue	Comes from personal name Donnachadh descending from 12th century King of Munster.
*1 *2 *3 Duff(e) – Dubh	Epithet surname of Dubh – also occurs as an abbreviated form of Duffin, MacElduff and Duffy.
*2 *3 Fowler	Means hunter of wild fowl. Most common in Dublin and Belfast. Sometimes substituted for Foley.
Hanley – Hanly – O'Hanley	Anglicised form of the Irish surname Ó hAinle, found principally in Connaught. Among their ancestors were two 11th century bishops of Dublin.
*3 Harris	An English surname adapted from the first name Harry. Came to Ireland at the plantation of Ulster in 1609.

[3] Kelly – Ó Ceallaigh	2nd most common Irish surname. It goes back over 1,000 years. May have come from the Irish word Cealleach (strife).
[2] [3] Lawless	An Anglo-Norman name meaning outlaw. They were one of the tribes of Kilkenny and are numerous in Dublin and Galway.
[3] Madden	Of Irish and English origin. Irish sept was a branch of Uí Maine (Hymani) living in Co. Galway. They once held estates in Mayo, Leitrim and Fermanagh. A Madden family of English origin came to Ireland in the 16th century.
[3] Maxwell	Scottish name came to Ireland with Cromwell's armies.
[2] [3] Moran	An Irish surname from Connaught. Two separate septs Ó Móráin and Ó Moghráin have both been anglicised to Moran.
[2] Monks – Ó Manacháin	Irish surname. The Manachain from whom the family takes its name was a famous Connaught warrior of the 9th century.
[2] [3] Murphy – Ó Murchú	Most numerous Irish surname Murchadh meant sea warrior. Three different septs.
[3] McCormack – MacCormaic	Irish surname formed from forename Cormac. Only sept of the name was from Fermanagh/ Longford area.
[2] [3] McKenna – MacCionnaith – MacFhionnaigh	Meaning son of the fair one, belonging to North Monaghan.
[1] [2] [3] Quinn – Ó Cuinn	From the personal name Conn. There were four distinct septs.
[3] Redmond	An Anglo-Norman surname mainly found in Wexford, Wicklow and Dublin.

[1] [2] [3] Reilly – Ó Raghailligh	One of the most numerous surnames in Ireland. At one time they ruled the network of lakes around Lough Erne. In the 15th century they devised their own coinage, giving rise to the saying *'Living the life of Reilly'*.
[3] Smith – Smyth – Mac Gabhann	Widespread Irish surname meaning son of the smith.
[1] [2] Tighe – Mac Teague	Anglicised form of Irish Surname Ó Taidhg. There were four unrelated septs, one in each province.
Wise – Wyse	Anglo-Norman surname. Prominent in Waterford city and county. Seen on the oldest stone in St. Pappan's graveyard dated 1691.

Names marked with '[1]' appear in the applotment book of 1823.
Names marked with '[2]' appear in Griffith's valuation of 1848.
Names marked with '[3]' are in the census of 1901 and 1911.

Headstones in St Pappans

Personalities, past and present

Henry Barry 1710 - 1751

Henry, fourth and last Lord Santry, succeeded to Santry estate in 1734. A prominent member of the notorious Hellfire Club, Henry was famous for his debauched life style. Dean Jonathan Swift spoke to Lady Barry about her wayward son but he was rebuked for his interference.

Drink was to be Henry's downfall. In August 1738 he stabbed Loughlin Murphy, porter at a Palmerstown public house[97]. Murphy died from his wounds. It was reported in court that Henry gave the innkeeper a £4 piece[98] before speeding from the scene. Henry was found guilty of murder by a court of his peers and sentenced to death[99].

Reprieve

The intervention of his uncle, Sir Compton Domville, is said to have saved Henry's life. Sir Compton threatened to cut off Dublin City's water supply, which ran through his Templeogue estate, unless Henry was freed. The death sentence was lifted. Henry lost his title and estates[100], and with his wife Anne Thornton, he left Ireland for Nottingham, never to return. Henry's debts were so enormous that an Act of Parliament was passed in 1741 to deal with them. However, later that year, he got a royal pardon and the regrant of his estate[101].

Life in exile

Henry's unhappy life in Nottingham can be glimpsed from his letters to friends in Ireland. Widowed in 1742 and childless, he complained of being *"greatly uneased"* at not hearing from Sir Compton or his aunts who ignored his letters. By 1748 he was in poor health, suffering from rheumatism and gout. Eventually, in 1748, correspondence with his uncle resumed. In 1750 Henry married Elizabeth Shore *'spinster of Nottingham'* [102] and died in March 1751. A grave was opened for him in Santry, but he was buried in Nottingham.

The story of the Dublin Hell-Fire Club, known locally as The Devil's Kitchen or simply the Hell-Fire Club it is inextricably linked to the infamous Dublin Hell-Fire Club.

At the beginning of the 18th century, there lived a class of gentry called "bucks" who spent their lives pursuing enjoyment in a most eccentric manner. Their behaviour was viewed at the time as an insult to the mot sacred principals of religion, an affront to Almighty God himself, and corrupting to the minds and morals of young people.

This life consisted it is said, of gambling, blaspheming, drinking, and even Satanism. The Dublin Hell-Fire Club was founded by Richard Parsons, 1st Earl of Rosse, and Colonel Jack St Leger. Jack St Leger, as his name suggests, had deep sporting instincts and his country house near Athy in County Kildare was the haunt of the leading gamblers and racing men of the day. Huge amounts of money changed hands at parties here, and vast quantities of liquor were consumed. It was in this atmosphere that the Dublin Hell-Fire Club was borne. Its motto was "do as you will".

The club had various headquarters around Dublin such as the now demolished Eagle Tavern on Cork Hill. On occasion at the Eagle, members would sit around a circular table upon which was placed a huge punch bowl of scaltheen, a mixture of Irish whiskey and melted butter.

Picture courtesy of National Gallery of Ireland

121

Lord Mayors of Dublin with Santry associations

Richard Barry - 1610[103]

Richard, father of James, first Lord Santry, lived at Toberbunny House which was owned by the Barrys 1641 - 1714.

Sir George Ribton 1747-1748[104]

As well as being Lord Mayor, Sir George was City Treasurer in 1749. He died in 1761 and was buried at St. Pappan's Santry.

John (Jack) Belton 1950-1951

Jack, a member of the Fine Gael party, owned Rose Cottage public house, Santry village, 1945 - 1950.

Patrick (Paddy) Dunne 1975-1976

Paddy, a member of the Labour party, was an active trade unionist. While working for the Dublin Port and Docks Board in 1968, he became branch secretary of the Workers' Union of Ireland. Paddy left the trade union movement in 1981. During his term of office Paddy was the first Lord Mayor of Dublin to be elected President of the capital cities of the E.E.C. (now E.U). He lived at Shanowen Ave., Santry from 1954. (Paddy Dunne died in 2006)

Patrick (Paddy) Belton 1978-1979

Paddy, a member of the Fine Gael party and T.D. for Dublin North East 1961 – 1979, was elected Lord Mayor in 1978. He served on a number of committees on Council, principally the Finance, Cultural and Selection committees. Paddy was a well known businessman. At the height of his business career he owned sixteen licensed premises throughout Dublin. Paddy, his wife Betty and family lived at *'Crestfield'*, Swords Rd., Santry 1957 - 1964.

Their home was knocked down to make way for factories and warehouses.

John (Jack) Belton
Lord Mayor of Dublin 1950-1951
Photograph courtesy of Dublin City Council

Patrick (Paddy) Dunne
Lord Mayor of Dublin 1975-1976
Photograph courtesy of Dublin City Council

Patrick (Paddy) Belton
Lord Mayor of Dublin 1978-1979
Photograph courtesy of Dublin City Council

Father Patrick Dineen (1860 - 1934)

Father Dineen, lexacographer and editor was born in Co. Kerry[105]. He became a Jesuit in 1894 but left the order in 1900 and devoted his life to writing solely through Irish.

In 1904 the first edition of his famous Irish - English dictionary was printed, followed by two much larger editions in 1927 and 1934[106]. In the early 1900s, Fr. Dineen lived at Royal Oak farm, Swords Rd., opposite Santry demesne. He often rambled by a ditch in the demesne which became known as "Dineen's ditch".

Pictiúr le caoinchead "Feasta"

Helen Roe

Helen Roe, teacher, librarian and renowned antiquarian lived at *"Coolfin"* Swords Road, Santry for almost fifty years.

During her lifetime, Helen became one of Ireland's leading experts on Irish High Crosses. In her eighties she wrote a booklet on the High Crosses at Monasterboice, which is still used today[107]. Between 1965 and 1968, she was first woman president of *"The Royal Society of Antiquaries in Ireland"*.

On her 90th birthday, the Royal Irish Academy presented Helen with a book in her honour entitled *"Figures from the past"* [108] a collection of articles by archaeologists and historians on the theme of figurative art in early Christian Ireland. Helen was thrilled to be so honoured in her lifetime.

After her death in 1988, Helen's home was bought by St. Michael's House and is now an adult residential care centre.

Helen Roe
© Reproduced by permission of
Royal Society of Antiquaries of Ireland

Monasterboice Cross
From "Monasterboice & Its
Monuments" by Helen Roe

Frank Hall

One of R.T.E's much loved personalities, Frank Hall came to Dublin from his native Newry in the fifties and settled with his family at Shanliss Rd., Santry.

Frank was a columnist with the Evening Herald before moving to R.T.E. where he presented his highly successful programme "Hall's Pictorial Weekly" from 1978 - 1988.

He was Film Censor from 23 October 1978 to 13 September 1986 and from 1975, wrote a weekly column for the Sunday World. Frank died in 1995 and is survived by his wife and four children.

Frank Hall
Picture courtesy of R.T.E. Guide

Sir A. J. F. O'Reilly

Tony O'Reilly, international businessman and rugby star, lived at "Auburn", Coolock Lane, Santry in his youth.

Tony played rugby for Ireland from 1955 - 1970, winning 29 caps, and toured successfully with the "British and Irish Lions" in 1955 and 1959.

He is chairman of Independent Newspapers and was a former manager of An Bord Bainne and the Irish Sugar Company and chairman of H. J. Heinz (International) from 1987 – 2000.

Picture courtesy of Murray Consultants

Mena Cribben

Our local postmistress, Mena Cribben, grew up in Santry demesne where her father, Matt Lawless, was land steward. She attended St. Pappin's primary school, Ballymun, and Scoil Chaitríona, Eccles St., and joined the civil service. Mena married Gus Cribben in 1956. They had six children.

Mena is a staunch traditional Catholic, whose love of learning and concern for her community have influenced her whole life. Her kitchen also serves as a classroom where local children are prepared, free of charge, for state examinations.

A talented musician and singer, Mena was organist and choir mistress at St. Pappin's Ballymun. Her choir continues to win awards at Oireachtas na Gaeilge. She also cares for "Ogras Naoimh Papain", a youth club for children from the Ballymun area.

Mena and Gus took over Santry post office in 1963. When the village cottage was demolished in 1973, they moved to "Coill Mhuire" Santry Ave. Sadly Gus died in 1999. Mena is no stranger to television having been a guest on the *"Late Late Show"* and taking part in recent documentaries. Her latest appearance was in the *"Would you Believe?"* series in a programme entitled *"The Wise Woman of the Woods"*.

Historic Walk
July 20th 2002

Santry Guild local history group were joined by other guild members and friends for a two hour walk visiting historic sites in the area.

Each participant was given a map of the proposed route prepared by Pat O'Looney. Group members answered questions on the various sites as recorded in our project.

It was a pleasant afternoon and we were all able to enjoy the flora and fauna *en route*.

Historic Walk.

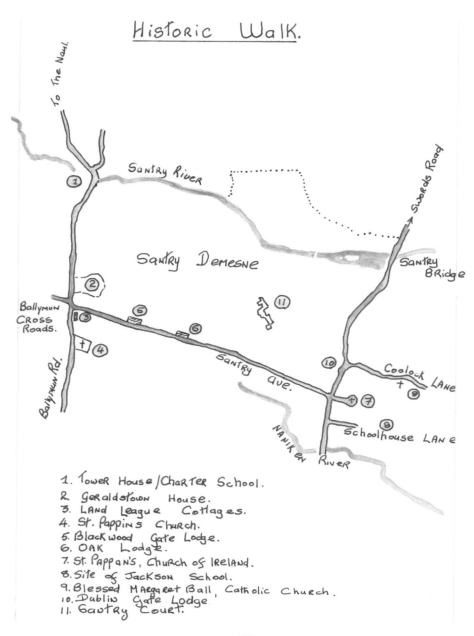

1. Tower House/Charter School.
2. Geraldstown House.
3. Land League Cottages.
4. St. Pappins Church.
5. Blackwood Gate Lodge.
6. Oak Lodge.
7. St. Pappan's, Church of Ireland.
8. Site of Jackson School.
9. Blessed Margaret Ball, Catholic Church.
10. Dublin Gate Lodge
11. Santry Court.

Acknowledgements

Maurice Ahern
Betty Barnwall
June Basagni
Elizabeth and Sarah Belton
Botanic Gardens (Colette Edwards)
Mena Cribben
Jim Cullen
Church of Ireland Library Archivist (Raymond Refaussé)
Edward Alan Domville
Dorothy Doolin
Ismail Dadabhay
Al Devine
Fás (Martin Kelly and Pat Murphy)
Aidan Farrelly
Ken Finlay (Southside Newspapers)
Mary Finn
Sheila Field
Fiona Fitzsimons
Peter Fowler
Dr. David Gray
Olive Hegarty
Patricia King
Yvonne Laidlaw
Billie McAnally
Rosaleen McCormack
Dermot McCabe
George McCullough
Tom McElroy
Ina McGinley
Joe Morgan
Mary Murphy
National Transport Museum (Michael Corcoran)
Anne Peters
Maria Prendiville
Antoinette Quinn (Biographer of Patrick Kavanagh)
Brendan and Doreen Scally

Sap Nurseries (Gráinne Murphy)
Professor Alan Smeaton
Swords Heritage Group (Bernadette Marks)
Anne Sheridan
Julie Tyrrell
The Bat Conservation Trust
Eva Walsh
Ray Walshe
Patricia York
Staff of: Dúchas
    National Archives
    Fingal Mobile Library
    National Library
    National Museum
    Irish Architectural Archives
    Dublin City Archives
    Library Trinity College Dublin
    Research Library Pearse Street

Maps

Rivers of Santry
1655 Survey
Santry Demesne 1812
Duncan's Map 1821
Ordnance Survey Map
Road Map - based on O.S.Map
Route of Historic Walk

Sponsors

Members of Santry Guild, I. C. A.
Aer Lingus Social and Athletic Association
Allied Irish Bank, Santry
Dublin City Council
Heritage Council
Mr W. Kilmurray

Notes

1. Adams, Rev. Benjamin, W. *History & Description of Santry & Cloghran Parishes 1883* p. 1
2. Ibid., p. 1
3. Store B3:15 National Museum of Ireland (Axe head)
4. Store D30:8 National Museum of Ireland (Flint Brass & Bronze)
5. Donnelly, Rev. Joseph, S. J. *Short Histories of Dublin Parishes* p. 2
6. Map F. P. 92 & 93 (section of) Sweeney Clair L. *The Rivers of Dublin.* 1991
7. O'Hanlon Rev. John Canon. *Lives of the Irish Saints* vol. VII pp. 440 - 442
8. Ibid., pp. 515 - 516
9. *Annals of the Four Masters* vol. I p. 443
10. Ibid., p. 442
11. Adams, Rev. Benjamin, W. *History & Description of Santry & Cloghran Parishes 1883* p. 22
12. Ibid., p. 1
13. Donnelly, Rev. Joseph, S. J. *Short Histories of Dublin Parishes* p. 15
14. Ibid., p. 15
15. O'Hanlon, Rev. John Canon, *Lives of the Irish Saints* vol. VII p. 517
16. *Calendar of documents relating to Ireland* 1285-1292 pp. 12 - 13
17. Donnelly, Rev. Joseph S. J. *Short Histories of Dublin Parishes* p. 16
18. Ibid., p. 16
19. Ibid., p. 16
20. Adams, Benjamin W. *History & Description of Santry & Cloghran Parishes 1883* p. 86
21. Simington, R. C. *The Civil Survey of Co Dublin 1654 - 1656* p. 196
22. Ibid., p. 202
23. Dalton, Dr. John *History of Co. Dublin* 1838 p. 130
24. *Complete Peerage* vol. I "Barry of Santry" p. 447
25. Simington, R. C. *The Civil Survey of Co Dublin* 1654 - 1656 p. 198
26. *Complete Peerage* vol. I "Barry of Santry" p. 448
27. Lewis, Samuel *A History & Topography of Dublin City & County* 1837 pp. 226 - 227
28. Walsh, Rev. Robert *Fingal & Its Churches* p. 231
29. *Complete Peerage* vol. I "Barry of Santry" p. 448 footnote B
30. Ibid., pp. 448 - 449
31. *Domvile Papers* Manuscript 235 National Library of Ireland
32. Joyce, Weston St. John *Neighbourhood of Dublin* p. 258
33. Adams, Rev. Benjamin W. *History & Description of Santry & Cloghran Parishes 1883* p. 94
34. Ibid., p. 94
35. Ibid., p. 19

36. Ibid., p. 92
37. Ibid., p. 93
38. Ibid., p. 26
39. Archer, Lieutenant Colonel Joseph *Statistical Survey of Dublin 1801* p. 208
40. Adams, Rev. Benjamin W. *History & Description of Santry & Cloghran Parishes 1883* pp. 1 - 2
41. O'Connell, Michael *Story & Guide to Fingal* pp. 40 - 41
42. Adams, Rev. Benjamin W. *History & Description of Santry & Cloghran Parishes 1883* p. 5
43. Ibid., p. 51
44. Archer, Lieutenant Colonel Joseph *Statistical Survey of Dublin 1801* p. 63
45. Ibid., p. 64
46. Domvile, Charles – Article entitled *Santry Estate* 1867 p. 1
47. Lewis, Samuel *A History & Topography of Dublin City & County 1837* p. 226
48. Chamley, Christopher and Mahon, James *Tythe Applotment Book for Santry* 1826 pp. 1 - 5 and MacOwen, Thomas and Phillips, William *Toberbunny Townland*
49. Domvile Lineage – *Domvile papers* Manuscripts 11864 and 11869 – National Library of Ireland
50. *Domvile Papers* Manuscript 9395 National Library of Ireland
51. Ibid.
52. Domville, Edward Alan *We came with the Conqueror* p. 118
53. Ibid., p. 121
54. Domvile, Lady Margaret *A Life of Lamartine* 1888
55. *Domvile Papers* Manuscripts 11864 and 11869 National Library of Ireland
56. *Act of Parliament* – Poë Name and Arms (Compton Domvile Estates Act, 1936) *Source: Irish Statutebook Database* 1922 - 1998
57. Information courtesy of Joe O'Connell, Dublin Bus (2001)
58. *Census of Ireland 1901* National Archives
59. *Times Pictorial Weekly* April 14th 1951
60. Information courtesy of George McCullough
61. Simington, R. C. *The Civil Survey of Co Dublin 1654 - 1656* p. 198
62. Map 16F 4 (1) 1812 *Domvile Papers* National Library of Ireland
63. Lewis, Samuel *A History & Topography of Dublin City & County 1837* p. 226
64. Ibid., p. 226
65. *Domvile Papers* Manuscript 9395 National Library of Ireland p. 14
66. *Domvile Papers* Manuscripts 11301&11935 National Library of Ireland
67. Fire on 24th October 1941 (Confirmed by Dublin City Fire Brigade)
68. Inscription on restored cover of Barry tomb St Pappan's Church, Santry. Restored by Alexander Ballantine (Resident of Santry Village 1847 – works based in Gardiner Street)
69. Adams, Rev. Benjamin W. *History & Description of Santry & Cloghran Parishes 1883* pp. 8 - 9

70. Ibid., p. 6
71. Bowe, Caron & Wynne *Gazatteer of Irish Stained Glass* p. 49
72. Adams, Rev. Benjamin W. *History & Description of Santry & Cloghran Parishes 1883* p. 3
73. Ibid., p. 19
74. Ibid., p. 37
75. Harvard, John *Report on Santry Charter School* 1825
76. W. J. McClelland of Santry Charter School highly recommended by the Board of the Incorporated Society at an Annual General Meeting in 1884. Signed A. S. Hart LL. D. Vice-Provost Trinity College Dublin (Chairman of the Board) and Rev. J. W. Hackett (Secretary) 73 Harcourt Street, Dublin 2
77. Adams, Rev. Benjamin W. *History & Description of Santry & Cloghran Parishes 1883* p. 2
78. Dalton, Dr. John *History of Co. Dublin* 1838 p. 131
79. Adams, Rev. Benjamin W. *History & Description of Santry & Cloghran Parishes 1883* p. 2
80. Ibid., p. 2
81. *Times Pictorial Weekly*, April 14th 1951
82. Ibid.
83. *Thoms Directories 1945 – 1985*, (Dublin: Alex Thom & Co.)
84. Adams, Rev. Benjamin W. *History & Description of Santry & Cloghran Parishes 1883* p. 32
85. Ballymun Guild, Irish Countrywomen's Association. *A History of Ballymun & Glasnevin 1985*
86. *Dublin Diocesan Guide Book* – Information courtesy of Dublin Diocesan Archivist, Robert Sheehy (2001)
87. *Inspector's Report*, 1907 National Archives of Ireland
88. Information from Maurice Ahern
89. Somerville-Woodward, Dr. Robert, *Ballymun A History (Synopsis)* p. 39
90. Lennon, Colm *The Lords of Dublin in the Age of the Reformation* p. 136
91. Ibid., p. 137
92. O'Donovan, John *Name Books for County Dublin* 1837 vol. IV
93. (Recorded) Dalton, Dr. John *A History of Co. Dublin* 1838, p. 133
94. (i) Patton, Linda, *National A.S.I. Survey (Santry Demesne) 19/8/1994*
    (ii) Goodwillie, Roger – *Preliminary report on the Flora & Fauna at Santry Demesne 24/9/1997*
    (iii) Curtis, Dr. Tom, et al. *Survey Santry Demesne 8/3/1999*
95. Goodwillie, Roger *Preliminary report on the Flora & Fauna at Santry Demesne 24/9/1997*
96. Curtis, Dr. Tom et al. *Survey of Santry Demesne 8/3/1999*
97. Gilbert, J. T. *History of Dublin City* vol. III p. 93
98. Ibid., p. 93

99.   Ibid., p. 95
100. *Complete Peerage* vol. I "Barry of Santry" pp. 448 - 449
101. Ibid., p. 449
102. Ibid., p. 449
103. Ibid., p. 447
104. Adams, Rev. Benjamin W. *History & Description of Santry & Cloghran Parishes 1883* p. 90
105. Boylan, Henry *A Dictionary of Irish Biography* p. 111
106. Ibid., p. 112
107. Roe, Helen M. *Monasterboice and its monuments*
108. Rynne, Etienne, Editor *Figures from the past – Studies of Figurative Art in Christian Ireland in honour of Helen Maybury Roe (Dublin: R.S.A.I. 1987)*

Bibliography

Aalen, F.H.A. and Whelan, Kevin   Articles Edited *Dublin City and County - Prehistoric to Present* (Dublin: Dublin Geography Publications, 1992)

Adams, Rev. Benjamin Wm. *History and Description of Santry and Cloghran Parishes 1883* (London: Mitchell and Hughes, 1883)

Appleyard, Douglas   *Greenfields Gone Forever* (Dublin: Coolock Select Vestry, 1985)

Archer, Lieutenant Colonel Joseph   *Statistical Survey of Co. Dublin 1801*   (Dublin: Graisberry and Campbell, 1801)

Archer, Patrick   *Fair Fingal*   (Dublin: An Taisce Fingal, 1992)

Bourkes Peerage (London: Bourke Peerage Ltd. in conjunction with Shaw Publishing, 1826)

Bowe, Caron and Wynne   *Gazetteer of Irish Stained Glass* (Dublin: The Irish Academic Press, 1988)

Calendar of Documents Relating to Ireland 1285 -1292. (Dublin: Alex Thom, 1879)

Census of Ireland, 1821-1911. National Archives of Ireland.

Complete Peerage Vol. 1, Barry of Santry (Glouster: Alan Sutton Publishing Ltd., reprinted, 1982)

Cosgrave, Dillon   *North Dublin City and Environs*   (Dublin: Four Courts Press Ltd., reprinted, 1977)

Dalton, Dr. John *History of County Dublin 1838* (Dublin: Hodges and Smith, 1838)

Domville Papers, Manuscripts 114, 235, 714, 9395, 11301, 11864, 11869, National Library of Ireland

Domville, Edward Alan *We Came With the Conqueror* (Southport: The Limited Edition Press, 1994)

Donnelly, Rev. Joseph S.J. *Short Histories of Dublin Parishes* (Dublin: Catholic Truth Society, 1915)

Fingal Heritage Group *Working Life in Fingal in the 20th Century* (Dublin: Fingal Heritage Group, 1994)

Gilberts Calendar of Ancient Records (Dublin: Joseph Dollard, 1892)

Griffith's Primary Valuation of Tenements (Santry Parish) (Dublin: Her Majesty's Stationery Office, 1848)

Joyce, Weston St. John *Neighbourhood of Dublin* (Dublin: Hughes and Hughes, 1912)

Lennon, Colm *The Lords of Dublin in the Age of the Reformation* (Dublin: Irish Academic Press, 1989)

Lewis, Samuel *A History and Topography of Dublin City and Country 1837* (Dublin and Cork: Mercier Press, 1980)

Mc Lysaght, Dr. Edward *Irish Surnames* (Edition V1) (Dublin: The Irish Academic Press, 1985)

O'Connell, Michael *Story and Guide to Fingal* (Dublin: Irish Holidays Ltd.)

O'Donovan, John *Annals of the Four Masters,* Vol.1 Edited from manuscripts in the Library of the R.I.A. and T.C.D. (Dublin: DeBurca Rare Books, 1990)

O'Donovan, John *Name Books for County Dublin,* Ordnance Survey Letters 196, Santry, Co. Dublin Vol. IV, (1837)

O'Hanlon, Rev. John Canon *Lives of the Irish Saints,* Vol.VII (Dublin and London: Duffy and Sons, 1873)

Petty, Sir William *Atlas of Ireland 1659* (Newcastle Upon Tyne: Frank Graham, reprinted 1968)

Ross, Craig Stella F.L.S. *Drawings of British Plants* (London: G. Bell and Sons Ltd., 1948)

Rutty, Dr. John *An Essay Towards a Natural History of Co. Dublin 1772,* Vol.II (Dublin: W Sleater, 1772)

Simington, R.C. *The Civil Survey of Co. Dublin 1654-1656,* Vol. VII (Dublin: Stationery Office, reprinted 1945)

Sweeney, Clair L. *Rivers of Dublin* (Dublin: Dublin Corporation, 1991)

Thoms Directories (Dublin: Pettigrew and Oulton, 1843) and (Dublin: Alex Thom and Co., 1945-1985)

Tythe Applotment 1823: Chamley, Christopher and Mahon, James, Santry Parish: (Lodged 18.9.1826) (Toberbunny Townland: MacOwen, Thomas and Phillips, William)

Walsh, Rev. Robert *Fingal and its Churches* (Dublin and London: William McGee, 1888)

Warburton, Whitelaw and Walsh *History of County Dublin* (London: T. Cadell and W. Davies, 1818)